W9-COL-853

THE SENSUOUS MAN

The Sensuous Man

by "M"

The first *how-to* book for the man who wants to be a *great* lover

LYLE STUART, INC. · NEW YORK

Library of Congress Catalog Card Number 71–150765

Published by Lyle Stuart, Inc.
Manufactured in the United States of America.

First printing: January, 1971
Second printing: February, 1971

Contents

1.

Becoming the Sensuous Man

I was twenty-eight years old before I *really* learned how to make love to a woman. And, by my reckoning, that means I wasted thirteen years. Thirteen years of embarrassment, disappointment, and frustration.

You couldn't pay me to turn back the clock. Today my sex life is adventurous, satisfying, full of variety. It's no accident that I am never without a warm, loving, and appreciative woman at my side.

For I became a Sensuous Man. To put it more accurately, I *learned* how to be a Sensuous Man. Any man can. We're all born with the ability to be sensuous. Unfortunately, very few men figure out the techniques that will enable them to become great lovers. That's what this book is all about—to help men who have not yet learned; who are unable to win, hold, and share the joys of sex with the women they so desperately desire.

Are you one of these men? If so, I hope to show you—

—how to banish premature ejaculation
—how to become expert at some of the great erotic techniques that have been known to superb lovers for centuries, such as The Velvet Buzz Saw, The Runaway Pinch, The Butterfly Flick, The Easy Rider, and other delights
—where to meet women
—how to master the art of prolonged lovemaking
—how to be a good sexual conversationalist
—how to achieve the ability to drive a woman almost insane with ecstasy

Is this book for you? Probably. Behind the bluster of most men is a fear of inadequacy, the suspicion that they don't really measure up in the sex department. We watch Sean Connery cavorting with women on the screen, or read the exploits of the erotically explosive characters in *The Carpetbaggers,* and we have to admit, secretly, that it has never been *quite* that good for us (whatever we tell our buddies). The sex life of the average guy is really pretty sad; and deep down he suspects that every other guy is doing better.

They aren't, most of them. Too many men make love like clods, heavy-handed and clumsy. Too many men are selfish and inconsiderate in bed. Too many men are incapable of the glorious achievement of bringing a woman to orgasm. And too many men are unable to satisfy even themselves.

My sex life was typical—founded on ignorance and restricted to clumsy grappling with girls even more ignorant than I. That quickie in the back seat of a '52 Ford never quite lived up to my expectations. It was mostly soggy clothes, messed-up lipstick, embarrassment, hurt feelings, and fear of discovery.

But that was yesterday. Today sex is an unending joy for me. What happened to change my appreciation of sex? Experience and luck. Mostly luck. I met several women knowledgeable enough to broaden my outlook and teach me a thing or two about both fucking *and* women. Sexually sophisticated themselves, they were candid with me, boosting my ego on the one hand while illuminating my shortcomings on the other. Under their patient and thorough instruction, I learned to *make* love without inhibition, to *receive* love without embarrassment, and to *give* love without restraint.

I will show you, step by step, how I became a better—some women say "the best"—sexual partner for a number of very exciting and sexually enlightened women. By the end of this book you should be a believer—and a sensational lover.

With tender hands, a probing tongue, an erect penis, and a wild imagination, a five-foot guy can feel ten feet tall to the women with whom he's making love. With practiced control of ejaculation, your confidence can be boosted to the point where you will be able to excite and delight the most sensuous woman. You can develop the techniques and the power to lead her into positions of infinite variety. And she will be not only willing, but thrilled to oblige and participate.

Let me help you unleash all the natural sexuality you have within you. Let me teach you how to satisfy a woman beyond her wildest dreams, and at the same time indulge yourself in incredibly pleasurable eroticism.

The Sensuous Woman will always seek out the Sensuous Man, for she knows that she will be raised to the ultimate plateau of sensuality.

You can be that man. Turn the page and start learning.

2.

Let's Bury the Myths

No man can realize his full potential as a lover if he thinks he is basically inferior material when it comes to sex. Many men have imagined handicaps which cripple them with women. They seem to feel that a man is either sexy or he ain't—and they *ain't*. It doesn't do any good to tell them that they can *learn* to be sexually proficient. They cling instead to a number of myths which convince them that they simply got a raw deal in life. "Where was I when they handed out good cocks?" they mutter in self-pity.

If you are the victim of such myths, wake up! Shake your head vigorously and clean up the mess that's inside. Your potential as a lover is as great as the next guy's—as soon as you kick away your psychological crutches. And that's what these myths are—excuses for failure. If I still believed in them, I'd be spending all my spare time gardening or writing letters to the editors of newspapers instead of enjoying sex.

This book discusses many such myths, which I hope to explode. But this chapter will explore the three that are most fundamental to the sexual anxieties of the average man.

Fags Need Good Bone Structure, but You Don't

One of the saddest things I've discovered over the years is that most guys think that good looks is 99 percent of the formula for sexual success. If you believe that, you are *wrong*, and if this book can convince you that you are wrong, then you will be well along the way to becoming a Sensuous Man.

More than anything else, sensuality is a state of mind. You can train your body physically for sex (and you will, if you follow the instructions in this book), but the key to good sex is in attitude, sensitivity, and knowledge—*all of which is in your mind.* If you are handsome to start with, so much the better. I am not so fortunate. But good looks is not the substance of sensuality. It is more like a lure—and there are many other lures, such as intelligence, good humor, wit, skill at games, musical proficiency, the ability to dance, the ability to carry on a lively conversation. *All* of these traits, by themselves and in combination with others, make you initially more attractive to women. You may not impress *every* woman. But as long as you've got *something* inside (a little heart, a little soul, a little intelligence), you will be able to find plenty of women who look for those qualities in a man. Too many handsome men never mature sexually because they feel secure on the basis of their looks—which are never enough to sustain a relationship with a woman—and neglect their inner qualities.

Some of the greatest male sex symbols of our generation, by way of example, could never be classified as "pretty boys." Humphrey Bogart? Marlon Brando? Yul Brynner? Jean-Paul Belmondo? Lee Marvin? The Beatles? Think about it. Aristotle Onassis must have a lot on the ball (and in his wallet, I suppose) to have won the world's most sought-after widow. Carlo Ponti doesn't seem to have much trouble keeping Sophia Loren at home. And Richard Burton, who bears a multitude of facial marks as a result of adolescent acne, has done all right for himself.

In short, fags need good bone structure (because beauty is 90 percent of the game in the gay world), but you don't. Look your best at all times, of course. But don't cop out because you think you aren't handsome enough—because you *are* (if *I* am, you are). And you may discover, whatever your other shortcomings, that sex is the one thing you're really good at. The world is full of unimpressive, quiet little guys who really know how to turn a woman on. When "J", the author of *The Sensuous Woman*, put together her list of the top ten "sexy" men, Dick Cavett was up at the top of the list. Women don't care that Cavett isn't six feet tall—they are entranced by his wit, his intelligence, and his self-deprecatory charm. And women would find the boyish Cavett sexy even if he *weren't* a star. He's got it.

The point is simply this: *Everybody is in the ball game—it's how you play that counts.*

Penis Size—When Is Enough Enough?

I know what many of you are thinking—"This pep talk is all well and good for most guys, but I have—er—a special problem." Your special problem is the most common source of sexual anxiety among men: *the fear that your penis is too small.*

How can your penis be too small? It reaches your body, doesn't it?

The number of men who share this feeling of inadequacy is all out of proportion to the number of men who have small penises, which shows how seriously most men take the supposed value of a large penis. But even the man with the small penis is unfounded in his fears. However glamorous or "manly" it may seem to be "well hung," penis size is not really a factor in intercourse. The size of a man's penis is not a central concern to a woman, who knows from experience that she is equally satisfied by any size, as long as the man wielding it knows what he's doing. (Besides, most women are too busy worrying about the size of their breasts to concentrate on *your* trivial fears.)

My favorite penis story (not that I collect them) concerns the two golfers coming in off the golf course on a hot day. The first golfer, a real little guy, says, "Com'on, Harry, let's go in and take a cold shower."

"Uh, no thanks, Charlie," his big, strapping friend says. "I'm in kind of a hurry."

"Aw, you've got plenty of time, it'll feel good."

"Yeah," Harry says uneasily, "but I—"

"For God's sake, man, it's a hundred degrees, you're soaking wet. You can't go home without a shower!"

"Well, to be perfectly honest, Charlie," Harry confesses in an embarrassed whisper, "I've got kind of a small penis. It doesn't look good in the shower."

"A big guy like you?" Charlie's jaw falls in astonishment. "You must be kidding!"

"No, it's real small," Harry says, head bowed.

"Well, listen—does it interfere with your sex life?"

"No," Harry admits. "I make love to my wife four times a week, and I have my secretary every day during the lunch hour. And then there's my mistress . . ."

"Listen," Charlie says, clapping Harry on the shoulder. "How would you like to trade yours for one that looks good in the shower?"

Anyway, if you are really neurotic and find yourself unable to laugh at your fears, consider these two points:

1. The difference in men's penis size is not so pronounced during erection. In other words, men whose penises are large in the flaccid state do not gain as much in size when they attain an erection; and a small penis grows proportionally larger. And you don't *really* care what it looks like in the shower, do you?
2. Whatever its size, the penis is not the primary instrument for arousing and satisfying a woman. Let's face it—penises don't have joints, they have no protruding surfaces, they are relatively inflexible when erect, and it takes a great deal of muscular effort to make them move even a little bit. You just can't do much with a penis except wave it around, bat it against something, or move it in and out. The *real* sexual organs, when it comes to making love to a woman, are the hands and the mouth. Whatever the size of your penis, it is worthy of its limited function, and it is fully capable of giving *you* pleasure as well.

Once you realize that you are not defective physically, you will have shot down one of your excuses for not being a good sex partner. But this deprivation will be well worth it, because you will have rid yourself of those self-defeating feelings of inadequacy which deprive many men of sexual fulfillment.

All I Ever Hear About Is Somebody Else's Action

One last word before I turn to the real stuff, the formula by which you can become the Sensuous Man. You may be suffering from a sexual inferiority complex because you have heard tall tales of sexual prowess that seems far beyond your reach. Dismiss these fantasies. In my experience, the best sexual encounters are to be found, not in bed, but in the lurid stories of loudmouths who bend your ear at parties, at the golf course, at business lunches, at the weekly poker game—wherever men get together and the talk turns to sex. I am as skeptical as the next guy when I hear the amorous exploits of some self-designated Lothario.

One fellow in particular sticks in my mind. My college baseball team had a first baseman I shall call Frank (since that was his name), who took great pains to make it clear that women considered him a first-rate lover. After practice, he would gather a tiny group of disciples in front of his locker and relate his experiences with his most recent date (always some girl from out of town, a coed from such-and-such state college). Frank was brash and good-looking, six-foot-two, muscular, and funny in a gross way (he could describe an erection in terms that would make a producer of stag films blush). His stories never failed to inspire awe in his eager audience, since each monologue invariably ended up with Frank's penis in the girl's mouth and his tongue between her legs. I mean, back then I thought it was a hell of an accomplishment to get a girl to French kiss and rub my back at the same time!

So Frank was our hero. And we needed one. For most of us, young and unsure of ourselves, sex was mostly frustration, anxiety, hard work, and idle dreams. But we could have our vicarious thrills by sharing in the legend of Frank, who told us that his sexual prowess left women numb with pleasure (after driving them absolutely wild, orgasm after orgasm).

Time passed and Frank graduated and went on to better things (selling encyclopedias in Santa Barbara). Through my usual strategy of flattery, gallantry, boundless enthusiasm, and barely contained lust, I found myself in bed one cold winter night with Sue, a slim blonde who interrupted my pitch by whispering in my ear, "Let's do it."

We did it, and after three successful and relatively satisfying tumbles under the covers (by my pre-Sensuous standards, at least), Sue rested in my arms and, with characteristic candor, related virtually *all* of her past sexual experiences—from the drugstore owner who felt her up when she was fourteen to the graduate student who had fucked her in the back seat of a Ford two nights before.

"And then I slept with Frank," she whispered halfway through her Homeric saga. I was all ears. How had our hero fared?

"He was the worst lay of my life," she said.

Poor old Frank. The moment he was alone with Sue, he froze up. She practically had to undress him; it took her the better part of an hour to bring him to an erection with her hand and her mouth; and, when he was finally stiff enough for penetration, he ejaculated between her thighs.

So much for Frank (and for Sue, the talky bitch). I only brought him up to counterbalance the Paul Bunyanesque notions that may be impeding your progress as a lover. If you follow the advice in this book, you should be the sexual equal of *any* man.

But remember, there's more to sex than simple technical proficiency. Some guys can turn on the charm and perform well, although mechanically, with almost every woman they meet. These are the guys who maintain the image of the "Don Juan." Are they happy? Not necessarily. Figure it out yourself: *If a man makes love to a different woman every night, doesn't it suggest that he has never experienced anything that made him want a woman for a second night, or a whole succession of nights?*

Don Juans may do incredible physical things with women, but the only satisfaction they get from sex is the feeling of conquest. Women are a challenge to men like this, and each sexual success is just an ego booster, another notch on the penis, as it were. But, at heart, these men don't really *like* women. They prefer the company of men, and they use their power over women to gain the respect of men. All their triumphs are hollow.

The object of this book is *not* to make you a Don Juan, a master of one-night stands. I assume that you *like* women, that you find their company stimulating and fulfilling, and that you want to establish sexual relationships with women on at least a semipermanent basis. The Sensuous Man has the knack of *enjoying* women. He respects his sexual partners and sees them as more than a means of banishing self-doubts about his masculinity.

Really good sex comes when a man and a woman have the time and inclination to explore each other fully and to learn to work together for mutual satisfaction. The truly Sensuous Man *needs* women to enrich his life, and he dedicates himself to the happiness and fulfillment of his bedmates.

If you are such a man, and if you are ready to make your entire body an instrument of sexuality, then read on.

3.

Laying the Foundation

Now that your head is on straight, let's open up training camp. First of all, we have to get into shape for sex. You rookies have to learn the fundamentals. And you *veterans*—the off-season has left you flabby and out of shape.

Actually, a strong physique is not that big a factor in love-making. Gentleness is more important than strength, grace more valuable than raw endurance. And the really critical muscles are in your fingers and tongue—not the biceps.

But there is enough physical exertion in intercourse to make a trained, healthy body a sexual plus. Good wind is important. A strong back reduces the likelihood of fatigue. And durable calves and thighs can permit you to indulge in a number of very stimulating and slightly acrobatic positions. Besides, a healthy body is more attractive to women.

I don't ask that you climb mountains, go jogging in blizzards, or run marine corps obstacle courses. Just get yourself in generally fit condition. But I want you to scrutinize the following suggested exercises very closely. Of special importance (because you have probably never given them a second thought) are the exercises that increase the strength and control of the tongue, and those that develop your tactile senses. I don't care if you *do* feel like an ass—*do them!* Everything you do to a woman and everything you *feel* are directed and experienced by your body. The more responsive and sensitive it is, the greater the pleasure both of you will derive from sex.

Exercises for Over-all Strength

SENSUALITY EXERCISE NUMBER 1

The first exercise, and the most difficult, is the familiar and hated push-up.

Lie down on the floor, muttering and cursing under your breath. Place the palms of your hands flat on the floor, approximately level with your shoulders. Keep your back straight and lift your trembling body off the floor to the full length of your arms. Then lower yourself to about one inch off the floor (you can touch the floor today, if you're really out of shape), and then push up again.

Start with five a day, if you can, and increase daily until you are doing ten to twenty push-ups regularly. Train yourself to feel guilty when you cheat or when you skip them altogether (I don't really *trust* you yet).

Besides being generally healthful and good for your character, push-ups will tone up your arm, shoulder, and hand muscles so you can sustain your weight for long periods of time in the male-superior "Missionary Position" (which I am going to try to get you to abandon later in the book).

SENSUALITY EXERCISE NUMBER 2

The next exercise, equally familiar to you, is running in place. Start by running in place thirty seconds—lifting those knees *high*—and work your way up to ten minutes.

Running in place tones up the whole body,

increases lung capacity, and (when extended laterally) provides you with a handy skill should you ever be discovered in the arms of a married woman by her irate husband.

If you live in a high-rise apartment building, do your running in place outside, sparing your downstairs neighbor's plaster, lighting fixtures, and nerves.

Exercises for the Pelvis

SENSUALITY EXERCISE NUMBER 3

Here's one you'd better do in private, since it slightly resembles a grizzly bear scratching himself by rubbing against a tree. Stand with your feet about eighteen inches apart, holding on to the back of a straight-back chair. Be comfortable, free of tension. Thrust your pelvis forward and back ten or twenty times—not rapidly, but steadily. Occasionally, in the forward-thrust position, rotate your hips slightly.

Now, pretend that you are listening to one of those ripple-muscled freaks crooning over the radio:

"Forward—back! Forward—back! Forward—back! *Upsee*-daisy, now forward—*rotate*—back . . ."

Do you realize that millions of housewives

spend countless hours every week carrying on like this?

Anyway, this exercise will strengthen your lower back muscles, enable you to penetrate deep into the vagina numerous times without tiring, and cause you acute embarrassment if you are caught at it.

SENSUALITY EXERCISE NUMBER 4

Lie flat on your back on the bed or on the floor. Spread your legs slightly and raise your knees, your feet flat on the surface. Now raise your pelvis, thrusting up and forward in one motion. Use your knees as hinges and your feet as the anchor for your up-and-forward thrust.

Try this exercise about a dozen times to start with, and increase to twenty-five. It will prepare your body for the female-superior positions (where the woman is astride you, "riding" your penis).

Tongue Exercises

SENSUALITY EXERCISE NUMBER 5

You can usually tell a good lover by his tongue. If a man can make his tongue flutter like the wings of a hummingbird, or use it to nail flying insects from across the room, then he has an erotic instrument of incredible value —particularly when it comes to tickling a woman's clitoris.

Here's your first tongue exercise: Stick it out. Now, keeping it stiff, move it from left to right like a windshield wiper, touching the edge of the mouth each time. Do this exercise for thirty seconds initially, and slowly work up to sixty seconds. An effective psychological aid for this one is to pretend that you're William F. Buckley, whose tongue would be marvelous for sex if it could be domesticated.

This exercise is specifically designed to prepare you for "The Velvet Buzz Saw."

SENSUALITY EXERCISE NUMBER 6

Stick your tongue out as far as it will go, then slide it back into your mouth as far as you can. Do this exercise ten times initially and work up to fifty.

The intent of this exercise is obvious.

SENSUALITY EXERCISE NUMBER 7

Fumble around in your kitchen cabinet until you find a whiskey shot glass. Leaving it empty (for now), cover your mouth with it as you would an oxygen mask, but don't press it against your face. Now slowly stick out your tongue as far as it will go without touching the sides of the glass. If you *do* touch the sides, withdraw your tongue and begin again. This time, elongate the tip of your tongue, making it more pointed, and try to go past the point where you last touched the glass.

This exercise serves a twofold purpose. In French kissing, your tongue should be pointed to explore her mouth and meet *her* tongue. Your tongue is larger than *hers*—if it's too broad when it enters her mouth, it may prove uncomfortable and frighten her.

Secondly, when stimulating the clitoris orally, the tip of your tongue should encircle the small shaft and only flick across the top of her clitoris.

If you don't understand this now, you will later.

SENSUALITY EXERCISE NUMBER 8

This one is no sweat. Place a small grape in your mouth. Keeping it between your teeth and your tongue, rotate it with your tongue. Be extremely careful not to break the skin of the grape. Roll it from side to side in your mouth and knead it with your lips.

When you are able to manipulate the grape in this fashion without rupturing the skin, then you are applying approximately the correct amount of pressure necessary to stimulate and excite her nipples without causing any pain to these very sensitive erogenous zones.

If you are able to bring the grape to an orgasm, so much the better.

Exercises for Tactile Senses

SENSUALITY EXERCISE NUMBER 9

This one may embarrass you a bit because it isn't in keeping with that tough, brawny, "stud" image. But it is *very* important training in the art of "feeling."

To make yourself more aware of your tactile faculties, gather together a number of household items with different textures, such as a fur pillow, a bar of soap, a cracker, a leather glove, your pocket handkerchief, a silk tie, a dish of tepid water, a slice of bread, and a suede teeshirt. Lay them out on a table, sit down in a comfortable chair, close your eyes, and slowly touch each item.

Now lean back in the chair and *remember* the feel of each item, trying not to feel like a complete idiot. Repeat the exercise until each one's special texture imprints itself on your fingertips and in your sensory memory.

Take this exercise seriously. A good lover has a keenly developed tactile sense.

SENSUALITY EXERCISE NUMBER 10

Finally, and most ludicrously, strip to the waist. Sit down at that same cluttered table with those identical items—and, with your eyes again closed, rub your body with each item. Again—stop, lean back, lick the bread crumbs off your fingers, and *remember* the feel of each item. You are training your entire body to be a discerning instrument of sensation.

When you have finished the exercise and your tactile sensitivity has been expanded and refined, strip the rest of the way down and go take a shower. You'll need it.

Oh, and by the way—*lock* your door before beginning this exercise. No sense *inviting* trouble.

4.

Getting It Up and Keeping It Up— Farewell to Premature Ejaculation, Inability to Ejaculate, and Impotence

The words that follow are, in many respects, the most critical ones in this book. The subject is impotence and premature ejaculation—sexual failure. But it goes deeper than that. And this section is required reading for you if you truly want to become accomplished in bed—even if you are not presently troubled by problems of sexual inadequacy.

You may wonder why I introduce this unpleasant subject so early—even before I give you the detailed and graphic instructions on "how to do it." The reasons are quite simple: Most men—even sexually "well-adjusted" men —have a sexual outlook and orientation which hinders them as effective lovers. It is this same outlook which is often responsible for impotence or premature ejaculation. And no man can experience the true potential joy of sex unless he is relatively free of the fears which burden so many of us.

Any knowledgeable male knows that the key to successful intercourse with a woman is his ability to attain an erect penis and to maintain that erection long enough to permit a mutually satisfying coupling. In simple terms, the man is concerned with "getting it up and keeping it up." This chapter is devoted to this paramount concern.

Secondly, and equally important, almost all men are faced, at one time or another, with an episode or two of impotence. The causes of this fleeting inability to attain an erection and satisfy a woman, as we shall see, are varied and perfectly natural (such as nerves, fear of discovery, or too much alcohol). But it's something that can happen to *any* man at *any* time. And if he isn't prepared for such a failure, he may misinterpret it, brood, panic, and whip himself up into such a state of anxiety that real, chronic impotence ensues.

So I exhort you—even if you have never failed to get a hard-on at the first smell of sex, and even if you have superb control of your ejaculation—to read the rest of this chapter. You may discover that there is a deeper pleasure to be found in the arms of your woman than you now enjoy.

First I will make a series of pertinent observations which relate to poor male sexual performance. Then we will get into the preventions and cures for sexual failure—including a virtually foolproof way to banish premature ejaculation from your sex life forever.

The Injustice of the "Double Standard"

We often hear about the unfairness of the "double standard" sexual ethic to women. Our selfish, male-oriented sexual mores are said to discriminate against women and deprive them of sexual fulfillment and freedom. All of which is probably true.

But we rarely hear about the other side of this coin. The double standard also places full responsibility for the success or failure of a sexual episode on the man. In a sense, a woman can never "fail" in bed. All she has to do is lie there and let the man do his stuff. A woman is never impotent. Frigid, yes; impotent, no. If she doesn't have an orgasm, we say "too bad," but we don't say "you failed." Furthermore, women can *fake* orgasm by writhing around, moaning and groaning, and heaving with mock ecstasy. Few men can tell a faked orgasm from the real thing.

Ah, but pity the poor male! Unless his dick gets hard, he can't do anything except fondle his woman and pray to the Goddess of Erection. And it's not something he can hide. His penis just rolls around like a limp sausage, mocking his masculinity. Impotence is humiliatingly obvious.

The same holds true for premature ejaculation. A man may insert his penis in his partner's vagina and then, in a frantic effort to "last," cease stroking, begin mumbling the day's stock quotations, and pinch his nose until it bleeds to distract him from sex—and still feel his sperm gushing out after only thirty seconds. Unless he is truly selfish and unaware, he knows that he has failed to satisfy his woman. He is a failure in her eyes—a *failure*.

The double standard is a double-edged sword.

Men Are Expected to Perform

The responsibility of the man to carry the burden of sexual success would be no great concern if we didn't place a high value on that success. But we do. Every young boy is taught that a man is supposed to be "masculine." And, as he becomes a teen-ager, he learns, through gossip, reading, and the media, that every real man is expected to be a good sexual performer. A boy begins to wonder if he measures up.

Even the word we use to describe a man's role in sex is a bit threatening—"performance." It's as if a man were on stage, proving himself in front of an audience. The average man, in fact, actually *thinks* of his sex partner as sort of an audience to his performance (and a critical audience, at that). When he's done, he asks, "How was I?"—if not literally, at least tacitly. The man feels pressured to perform well, and if the pressure is strong enough he may be so fearful and distracted that he will be unable to achieve an erection.

A few episodes of this nature, coupled with

the man's concept of what society considers good sexual performance, and he begins to think of himself as something less than a man. He is impotent. There is nothing physically wrong with him, but the combination of his fears and the "audience's" expectations soon makes him a sexual wreck and a miserable human being.

Sex Is Not Competitive

Most men look at sex as if it were not only a performance, but a contest as well. When they aren't asking "How was I?" they're asking (or thinking), "Was I better than George?" Usually the opponent is the imagined "typical American male," a mythical male-image whose exploits have to be topped. Sometimes the opponent is the guy or guys who have had sex with his woman before he came along (which is why some men insist on virgins for wives—they are afraid of losing).

And sometimes the opponent is the woman herself! There are couples who make love like it was a death rite, playing the roles of the savage, conquering male and the bitter, emasculating female. But who wins?

Never lose sight, as you progress in this book,

that the object of sex is not to be good, better, or best at it—the object is to derive enjoyment from it. And the odds are that the more competitive you are when you fuck, the less pleasure you derive. There is no Super-Bowl of Sex, so don't concentrate on how good you are compared to some other guy. Concentrate on your pleasure and your lady's pleasure. That's the only way you'll emerge a "winner."

Fear Is the Enemy

All the points I've discussed up to now result, in most men, in sexual anxiety. But in some men the result is outright *fear.* The burden of performance proves to be too much for them and they become impotent.

The classic example is the young boy, sexually naïve, whose friends pressure him into visiting a prostitute in a run-down neighborhood. The room is filthy and the whore is an old hag. Her appearance is so repulsive and her approach so demanding that the boy freezes up. Sensing his confusion and ignorance, she begins to deride his manhood while flaunting her body at him, until finally he flees in humiliation, her laughter ringing in his ears.

From that day on, every opportunity to have

sex with a woman is a threatening situation. He is paralyzed by anxiety and his woman usually grows impatient. Instead of being understanding and sympathetic, she may demand, "What's the *matter* with you?" And, after a few such failures, even a warm, loving, understanding woman is unable to overcome his fears of failure and his distaste for sex. His sex life becomes a horror story.

A more common instance of impotence occurs when the wife or girl friend of a premature ejaculator finally makes known her dissatisfaction with his performance. He may never have had trouble getting an erection *before,* but that was before sex became something he had to struggle with. Now his partner demands more staying power. He tries to control himself, but fails. He resorts to all sorts of tricks and gimmicks, but fails. And his understandably frustrated lady begins to question his masculinity.

So does *he*. Before long, he is trying so hard to satisfy *her* that sex becomes a chore. He begins to anticipate failure, and he dreads the argument that will follow. Soon he is making excuses to *avoid* sex. And if, when they try to make it, he can't get an erection any more, he says he's just tired.

But he isn't tired—he's scared. He's scared

because he thinks he's a lousy lover. He's scared because he senses that he's getting worse. And he's scared because his partner is contributing to his anxieties in her eagerness for long-overdue sexual fulfillment.

Finally, you have an impotent male. He's just as bad off as the kid who *never* made it, even though he was once fully capable of erection and ejaculation with a woman. He has scared himself sexless.

How to Prevent Impotence

Let's assume that you are just an average guy. You have had no major sexual traumas in your life, and you have what could be called a "typical" sex life. Here's what you can do to prevent yourself from ever becoming impotent:

1. First of all, don't read this chapter ten times if you're doing well already. Thinking about impotence too much might cause you to worry about it, and worrying about it is what *causes* it. Some guys have a marvelous talent for messing themselves up.
2. Accept the fact that *every* man fails occasionally. Don't get nervous because you fall into the sack one night, ready to screw your mate, and can't. You may be physically ex-

hausted. You may have had too much to drink. You may be distracted by some important nonsexual event that is monopolizing your thoughts. Or you may simply be in one of those periods when you just aren't as horny as usual. *Anything* that distracts you from sex will cause you to have difficulty in attaining an erection. Don't worry about it, it's perfectly natural. It does *not* mean that you're impotent.

3. Make your sex life noncompetitive. This calls for real communication with your partner. You must direct your sexual episodes toward mutual fulfillment. The only object of your sex play must be giving each other pleasure. If either of you is trying to "prove something" in bed, then the situation is fraught with danger. Sooner or later, one of you will begin to frustrate, disappoint, and finally *fail* the other.
4. Learn how to satisfy your woman. That will rid you of your greatest source of anxiety: being judged and found wanting. If your problem is premature ejaculation, cure yourself (I will tell you how later in this chapter). Learning to control your ejaculation is essential to your future sexual relationship.
5. "Lighten" your sex life. Learn to laugh about sex, and don't let *her* take it too seriously either. It's supposed to be *fun,* not something you brood about.

If you follow this advice and maintain a cheery, open, and honest disposition about sex, there is little likelihood that you will ever become impotent—because sex will never be the source of any real anxiety.

How to Cure Impotence

If you are already impotent—or if you are just experiencing increased difficulty in "getting it up"—you will have to accept the fact that you cannot fix it all up just by trying harder, or by concentrating more. The exact opposite is the case. The more you try to *force* your penis erect, the less likely it is to happen.

A penis does not achieve its erect state because a man "wills" it to do so. It stiffens naturally and without conscious effort when a man becomes sexually excited. But . . . if that same man is *thinking* about it getting stiff, and fearing that it won't, then that distracts him from whatever was exciting him sexually in the first place, and it *won't,* just as it wouldn't if he were thinking about some neutral subject, like soybeans. To put it more graphically, if a woman is kissing your neck and stroking your penis, it will normally become erect. It feels good, she is appealing, you become excited. But if, instead, you are afraid that she will think you are an inferior lover and won't satisfy her, then you will be brooding and fretting about that (just the way you fret about going to the dentist). The result? No excitement, no arousal, no erection.

There is nothing you can do to *make* an erection. There are no exercises. There are no mental gimmicks. There are no electrical stimulators or other gadgets that will do the job.

The only way for you to cure impotence is to learn to relax and let nature take its course. That may sound simple enough, but nobody can make you relax by shouting in your ear, "Relax, relax!" It means that you have to completely restructure your attitudes about sex. It means that you have to rid yourself of all the fears and misguided goals that cause you anxiety. And it means you have to work together with a sex partner who will assist in this transformation to a totally new sex orientation.

If you have *always* been impotent, this do-it-yourself approach to curing impotence will probably not be enough. Your difficulty is likely a reflection of a very old and deep-rooted sexual anxiety, perhaps influenced by rigid religious training. If so, you should seek psychiatric help to get at the core of your problem.

But, if your difficulty in getting an erection is

a more recent phenomenon, then you have a very good chance of fixing yourself up (although professional guidance by trained, reputable counselors may still be advisable).

First of all, you can't do it by yourself. Masturbation is a no-threat situation, so jacking off doesn't solve your problem. No, you have to have a female partner. She must be sensitive and sympathetic. She must *know* what you are trying to accomplish. And she must be devoted to that end, even if it means temporarily forsaking her own sexual satisfactions.

The object of your efforts is to take *all* the threat out of your sex life, thereby eliminating the anxieties that prevent erection. You do this by indulging in sex play with your partner that is completely undemanding. Her role is crucial. She must make it clear to you that she is happy just to touch you and be close to you. She must convince you that she is *not* demanding sexual release during these sessions. And she must convince you that even the presence or absence of your erection is unimportant.

All that matters is touching, talking, and giving pleasure. No effort should be made to get a hard-on. And, if you do get one, *don't* try to use it! Make no effort to copulate to orgasm. That would be self-defeating, since you would just be trying to "beat the clock" again, and the distraction would make your erection disappear.

As your days of nondemanding touching in bed progress, you will probably begin to achieve erections (assuming you aren't staring at your penis, praying for an erection to happen). That will occur when you are fully satisfied that you don't *have* to have one to please either yourself or your partner. And when you get it, don't worry about losing it. Let it go limp. It's gone? So what? (It's a good idea to intentionally distract yourself, letting it go limp, and then letting your lady tease it up again with her fingers or lips. Do that over and over again. Soon you'll recognize that you don't have to worry about getting another erection when this one is gone.)

The next step is for your partner, in the female-superior position, to insert your newly erect penis in her vagina. She should put it in herself, rather than allowing you to become distracted from the pleasurable sensations. She should not thrust at this time, because that would be too demanding and would scare away the erection.

If you *do* lose it, fine. Don't worry—just start over. As you gain more confidence, you can begin to stroke your penis back and forth in her wet but motionless vagina—purely for your own enjoyment. She should be satisfied, at this point, with knowing that you are making progress and that it feels good to you.

After a few episodes of this nature, you may be able to use her vagina to bring yourself to orgasm. But the important thing to remember is: *Don't work for it!* It should not be the goal of your love-making—just a happy result of circumstances.

The more confident you are that you can maintain an erection for a reasonable length of time, and achieve another one later, the more she will be able to progress as an active participant. She will be able to thrust against your penis without your feeling threatened. And finally, and triumphantly, the two of you will be able to make love together with complete abandon—free of anxiety and with no misguided goals or challenges except your delight in making each other happy.

I strongly urge that, before you undertake such a mutual effort at sexual salvage, you buy a copy of *Human Sexual Inadequacy* by Masters and Johnson, from which I have drawn several of the specific recommendations in this chapter. Their much more detailed and sophisticated survey of the subject should benefit you immensely.

Advice to the Potent Male

Make sure you understand the philosophy behind the cure for the impotent man I have just described. Even if you have no problem getting a hard-on, the anxiety-free frame of mind is very important to your happiness and effectiveness as a lover.

I even recommend that you indulge in "non-demanding" sex play with your woman every now and then—abandoning orgasm as a goal for one session. Touching and talking with no effort being made to achieve a specific goal can affirm the nonthreatening, mutual devotion of your relationship. It should be a rewarding exchange. And the next time you can fuck yourselves silly.

The Causes of Premature Ejaculation

Premature ejaculation ("coming" too soon to satisfy the female) seems to be an unfortunate pattern developed early in a man's sex life. Many men, while still teen-agers, are conditioned to a quick release by visiting prostitutes, whose chief interest is not sexual fulfillment, but quick turnover. Whores sometimes try to outdo each other at "squeezing the juice out of a man" in the shortest possible time. And men, to please the prostitute, have often complied—wham-bang and it's over!

Another influence may be a boy's need for privacy when he masturbates. Fearing discovery, or the possibility of arousing his parents' suspicions, he tries to come as quickly as possible when he masturbates in the bathroom. And slowly but surely he trains himself to do exactly that.

Well, there's nothing wrong with a quick orgasm if you're masturbating or screwing a prostitute. But when you're trying to make *love* to a woman and satisfy her sexually as well, then it's a major disaster. The woman wants to come to an orgasm when she has your penis in her vagina but, if you shoot your wad after only a few quick pumps, she won't have time. Unable to relieve her sexual tensions, she will experience great frustration. You—being an aware, sensitive male—would still bring her to climax with your hands or mouth—but the two of you can't really get the most out of your sex life unless you can prolong your intercourse long enough for her to have an orgasm (or lots of orgasms).

A man's inability to withhold ejaculation long enough to satisfy his girl causes him no real trauma until she rightly calls his attention to the fact that *she* has feelings too. Many women *never* speak up. Some don't because they don't realize that they are entitled to sexual pleasure just as men are. Some remain silent because they believe that unpleasantness and martyrdom are simply a woman's lot. And some never speak out because they were raised to believe that sex is something distasteful—and the sooner over with, the better.

But most women desire sexual fulfillment and suffer greatly when their lovers mount them, ejaculate in seconds, and then roll over and go to sleep. There isn't too much hope for the girl friend of this sort of man—he probably thinks he's a great lover ("fucked her good, man!").

Almost as sad is the case of the guy who *is* sensitive to his gal's desires, but just can't help himself. He tries every gimmick in the book to prolong intercourse, including:

—Masturbating an hour before making love.

—Spraying his penis with a local anesthetic to reduce the sensation.

—Wearing an unnecessary condom (or *two*).
—Urging his partner to avoid all contact with his penis until insertion, lest he ejaculate outside her vagina.
—Trying to make his mind a blank, or concentrating on baseball scores or other nonsexual interests.
—Pulling his hair or biting himself to distract his mind from the pleasurable sensations.

His efforts are almost always in vain. But even if they worked it would still be lousy sex. A man *wants* to have his penis stroked, and his mind *should* be on sex, not baseball scores. At best, with an understanding woman, the premature ejaculator is miserable. At worst, with a woman who constantly nags him about his inability to control himself, he becomes impotent.

How to Banish Premature Ejaculation

Fortunately, in contrast to impotence, premature ejaculation is largely a *physical* distress. Which is not to say that you can just will it away, or take a pill, but it is subject to direct conditioning. In other words, you can *train* yourself not to ejaculate prematurely. You can learn control.

As in dealing with impotence, the female must be a full partner in the "cure." Once again she must temporarily sacrifice her own eagerness for sexual release in the best interests of your future relationship.

The technique for controlling ejaculation (again, presented in *Human Sexual Inadequacy* in more detail) is the "squeeze technique." The woman sits on the bed, her back against the headboard and her legs spread. You lie on your back, your head at her feet, your pelvis between her legs, and your legs over hers. This provides her with easy access to your penis.

As soon as she has brought you to a full erection, she should apply the "squeeze." She does this by placing her thumb on the frenulum of the penis (the "underside" of the penis, or the side facing her) and the first and second fingers on either side of the ridge formed by the glans on the *other* side of the penis. (She should grip your penis as if it were a shot glass and she were about to take a drink.) Then she squeezes her thumb and first two fingers—hard—for three to four seconds.

Every time she does this you will be surprised to discover that you will immediately lose your urge to ejaculate. You may lose a bit of your erection, but don't worry about that. After about thirty seconds she can begin stroking you again. Once you've reattained full erection, the squeeze is repeated. And so on. You can go on almost indefinitely this way without an ejaculation, but on the first attempt limit yourself to four or five times.

As you progress, she will be able to judge from your responses when to apply the squeeze. And, for perhaps the first time in your life, you will be maintaining an erection for longer periods of time without ejaculating.

After a few days of the squeeze technique, you can move on to "nondemanding penetration." She should mount you with her knees at about your nipple line. By leaning over you at a forty-five-degree angle, she can easily insert your penis and slide back on it. She should retain your penis in her vagina *without moving.* You are now permitted the wonderful sensation of penetration without having to worry about fucking her or lasting. If you feel yourself starting to come, tell her so immediately. She can lift herself off your penis, apply the squeeze to prevent ejaculation, and then reinsert the penis.

After a few more days, you can begin to thrust your penis in the vagina, although she should not respond with rapid thrusting of her own. Then, as your control increases, she can begin to thrust with you—slowly. And, before long, you will be able to copulate normally and without taking your mind off sex. Stick with female-superior positions, however (details to come in Chapter 8)—control is more difficult with the male on top.

It is important to continue with the squeeze technique for some time—at least once a week—although most of your couplings can be completely natural and spontaneous. But this helps create an indelible pattern of control in your ejaculation process.

I recommend, however, that you seek professional counseling when employing the squeeze technique. Not because there's any danger; not because it doesn't work—but because you may become impatient after your early successes and try to progress too rapidly. A competent counselor can assure that you are doing yourself the most good in the least time.

I don't have to tell you how happy you'll be when you've mastered prolonged control. By altering your pattern of ejaculation, you will be able to use your penis as an erotic instrument, bringing your partner to orgasm after orgasm. Control is great for its own sake because it brings you prolonged sexual pleasure, but for your lady it's even more than that—it's the door to her equal participation and sexual fulfillment.

And with that out of the way, the rest is icing on the cake.

5.

Do We or Don't We? The Ins and Outs of Masturbation

I have a friend who insists that the most exciting sexual act he knows is sitting on a bed with a woman, the lights on, and watching each other masturbate.

"It *has* to be exciting," he says. "Masturbation is the one thing that all men are ashamed of, or at least embarrassed about. So jacking off while my woman watches really turns me on. It's so *unacceptable.* We just revel in our degradation."

My friend is a nut, of course. He makes a lot of money being nutty for audiences. But his comment is still a valid testimonial for that much-maligned source of erotic pleasure—masturbation.

Masturbation is pretty much the same as any other kind of sex, except that you don't *usually* have company. Therein lie its shortcomings and virtues.

First its virtues:

1. It ends in orgasm. And orgasm feels great any time—at home in bed with your wife or in the rest room of a Greyhound bus rolling down the Interstate.
2. It is a physical and emotional release—a means of easing tension.
3. It is available to all, whatever their physical appearance or personality problems—the most democratic and egalitarian sex act.
4. It is private.
5. It requires no other party. No reservations, no table settings—you don't even need furniture.
6. It is easily performed while standing up.
7. It is quick—no complicated and time-consuming foreplay is required to excite a part-

ner, and after orgasm there is no need to pass a half hour or so in social amenities.

8. There is no pressure to "perform" well.
9. It is almost *always* available, requiring only a degree of privacy.
10. It is uncomplicated—no arguments, cajoling, hypocrisy, bargaining, or deception of another party. The simplest sexual act.
11. It is free of disheartening and calamitous consequences, such as venereal disease and pregnancy.

Now for the defects of masturbation:

1. It can leave crusty little stains on your sheets, your toilet seat, or your catcher's mitt.
2. It does not widen your circle of acquaintances.
3. It can strengthen the muscles of your right hand and wrist at the expense of your left hand and wrist.
4. You may be discovered masturbating in some semipublic refuge. Very embarrassing.
5. You may become obsessed with setting records for distance of ejaculation and volume of discharge.
6. It doesn't add to your store of gossip.
7. It is somewhat lacking in variety (Portnoy to the contrary).

When you weigh the virtues of masturbation against the defects, the case *for* masturbation is by far the stronger.

Not that it *needs* a case. Every adolescent male engages in the practice to what he thinks to be "excess," and most men continue to masturbate throughout their lives when other sexual outlets are not available. And when you consider that, until just recently, most boys were brought up to believe that masturbation was a form of "self-abuse" that led to madness, physical frailty, pimples, and blemishes, you begin to appreciate the irresistible appeal that jacking off must have for males who don't have a convenient vagina in which to ejaculate.

Consider the attitude of the boy whose mother discovered him masturbating. "Stop that this instant," she shrieked, "or you'll go blind!" The son, a good lad who wanted to please his mother, answered, "Can I just do it till I need glasses?"

Not only has masturbation been a "sin" for centuries, but scientists and theologians over the years have linked the practice, beyond refutation, to witchcraft, leprosy, rock music, communism, schizophrenia, athlete's foot, stunted growth, and the national debt. Masturbation has been a very convenient scapegoat. Most of the ills of the body, the mind, and society have been attributed to its malignant influences.

Today we are enlightened, of course, and doctors and priests tell us that masturbation is perfectly all right as long as we don't do it *too often,* or like it *too much,* and as long as we recognize that it isn't *as good* or *as healthy* as intercourse with a woman.

The result of this ambiguity about masturbation is that most men and boys are still a bit ashamed because they indulge in the practice. I mean, they will subscribe to the statement that just about all men masturbate at one time or another, but they will stutter and stammer and make evasive statements if you ask them if *they* masturbate. And these are often the same guys who are most articulate about their sexual exploits with women.

I remember quite vividly an episode that occurred the very first day I was in the army. About two thousand of us recruits were paraded into a large assembly hall and a medical officer took the stage, introduced himself, and asked the following question: "How many men in this hall have masturbated?"

There was an instantaneous murmur, and a couple of hands went up of guys who were mostly just trying to be funny, whereupon the captain roared: "Exactly 95 percent of all the men in this room have masturbated. And the other 5 percent are liars."

So men continue universally to jack off, and continue to feel guilty—or at least silly—because they do. Here are a few of the notions about masturbation that worry men:

1. *I may be doing it too much. I'll get run-down.* The answer to this, in physical terms, is simple. It is impossible to masturbate *too much,* just as it is impossible to fuck too much. If your body is exhausted or your mind is distracted, you won't be able to get an erection. So relax. If you've got a hard-on and you feel like having an orgasm, go ahead. Your body is saying *yes.* And don't be dismayed because you read that twice a week is normal, or once a day is normal. Everybody is different and nothing is normal. Nobody says a guy is sick if he can fuck his wife fifteen or twenty times a week—they just call him "Superman." The same goes for masturbating. If you want to jack off five times a day, and you *can,* then do it. You aren't masturbating too much until you start missing appointments and skipping meals.
2. *It's antisocial.* Rubbish. And, even if it were, so what? Who says you have to be social all the time? Many people in our "other-di-

rected," acceptance-seeking society are outraged by any act which an individual does not share with his fellow man. They consider masturbation (or not marrying, or even being a mild nonconformist) as a form of narcissism or "self-love." My answer is that each of us is an individual personality; we come out of the womb one at a time; and there is nothing immoral, harmful, or antisocial about enjoying something by ourselves.

3. *If I masturbate a lot, I will become an introvert.* If this were true, I would recommend masturbation to most of my Hollywood friends. A little introversion would do them good. But this is a logical fallacy. Withdrawn, shy men may be steady masturbators, but this does not mean that they became introverts *because* they masturbated. Extroverts masturbate too.
4. *I understand that the sexual fantasies associated with masturbation are unhealthy.* This notion is currently popular with a number of sex "experts." Whipping it off is okay, they say, but look out for those dirty thoughts! You may get hooked on your fantasies and turn away from reality. Well, I'm no expert, but I know that most men *need* their fantasies to reach orgasm. What other sexual stimulus is there in masturbation besides your imagination? Unless you are very easily aroused,

your hand certainly isn't enough. The sexual daydreams that accompany masturbation are perfectly healthy. And usually, the more exciting the fantasy, the better the ejaculation. Let your imagination go!

5. *I might get to like it too much.* What's wrong with liking it? You *should* like it. The more you like it the better. The residue of Puritanism is still with us—we feel guilty when we enjoy something. But only a fool or a fanatic limits his capacity for harmless pleasure.
6. *It isn't as good as sex with a woman.* So what? Nobody's asking you to substitute masturbation for heterosexual relations. It's just a very satisfying sexual release when a female partner is not available. Tuna fish isn't as good as lobster, but that's no reason you can't enjoy *both.*

In short, masturbation is terrific. There is no need to downgrade it or apologize for it. After all, the penis is a very ignorant organ. It can't tell a mouth from an anus or a hand from a vagina. It just wants to be rubbed while your brain is being stimulated erotically—and it rewards you with an incredible feeling of pleasure and release.

Masturbation is an enjoyable act which you can practice for the rest of your life. It is one of our greatest tension-relievers. And it is completely harmless to self and society.

Except, of course, that your ears will fall off.*

---

* *Note to the literal-minded:* Disregard the final paragraph. He's only kidding.—Ed.

6.

Where to Meet Women

The Sensuous Man is based on what may be an unwarranted assumption—that you have one or several women with whom you indulge in the ordinary, extraordinary, and altogether delightful practices described in this book. After all, what good is all this knowledge if you don't have a woman? You've practiced every exercise, banished all inhibitions, increased your sensitivity, and perfected your sexual technique—

and then you're sitting alone in your pad, fairly *bursting* with excess sensuality.

What am I supposed to do for you then? Write *The Sensuous Hermit?* The prospect of a Sensuous Man without a woman recalls the words of Dr. Frankenstein: "Good God, I've created a monster." So let's get to work on the problem of finding you a suitable bedmate if you lack one.

Before we begin, let me preface these guidelines with an uplifting note and a discouraging note.

First the good news: There are more women than men in the United States. Obviously there are more than enough to take care of every sex-crazed man.

Now the bad news: The reason there are more women than men is mostly that they *outlive* us—so a good percentage of your prospects are over seventy years old.

So much for the so-called surplus. We can define your "field of possibilities" more narrowly by eliminating from consideration the very elderly, the very young (let's say fifteen and under, but watch your step), the criminally insane, the terminally ill, hard-drug users and alcoholics (unless you are a masochist, male nurse, or humanitarian), dedicated prostitutes, and members of the DAR. Next we eliminate spinsters, confirmed lesbians, and Women's-Lib militants. And finally we rule out, for the sake of argument, those women who are already married.

What do we have? My hasty calculations, by no means definitive, indicate that there are still plenty of women perfectly suited to a man *just like you.*

A Heretofore Unrevealed Secret Technique for Meeting Available Women

Believe me, there *are* available women who will be compatible with your personality, susceptible to your sensuality, and receptive to your advances. The best evidence of this is the number of articles and books for women on the subject, "Where to Meet Men" (also titled, "How to Catch a Man"). There are as many women hunting men as the reverse, and probably *more,* since many women worry about getting married before it is "too late." The only difference is, most women don't hunt as openly, even though the stakes are often higher for them.

My first advice, then, for the man who wants to meet prospective sexual partners, is this:

Buy several women's magazines and a book or two (such as *The Sensuous Woman* or *Sex and the Single Girl*). Turn to the sections on "Where to Meet Men," find out where available men are supposed to be found, and *go there.*

The women will be waiting for you. Look for the carefully dressed ones, in singles and in pairs—particularly the ones who crane their necks to check out each new arrival at a "singles" bar, who stare endlessly at unfathomable abstract sculpture at the museum, or who feed pigeons in the park until the glutted birds topple on the sidewalk belching popcorn and bread crumbs. Such women can be approached with confidence.

The Pickup

If you can get *at* a woman, you have at least a chance of getting *into* her. And since most women in our society are "at large"—free to move about in public without restriction—any reasonably attractive man with a fair degree of brashness has a good chance of scoring with a complete stranger. It's simply a matter of his insinuating himself into her affairs as unobtrusively and charmingly as possible and then taking advantage of the already-established acquaintance. In simpler terms, giving her a line and seeing if she bites.

Are you cool enough to pick up a girl? Most men, in truth, are not. But, if you are, the opportunities are limitless. You can approach women on the street, in department stores, in bars and restaurants, at parties, on busses, on airplanes (particularly that most respectable pickup, the stewardess), at tennis matches, in elevators, at the laundromat, in the frozen foods section, in the park, and, of course, the classic—at the museum.

The secret of success in picking up women is "the line." It must be credible; or, on the other hand, so incredible and outrageous as to be amusing and appealing. It should be smooth enough to disguise inner fears or alarming lust, but not so flashy or phony that it smacks of insincerity or vulgarity. And it should have a built-in time-limiting factor—a line should be of short duration. Avoid any fabrications that have to be sustained throughout the relationship. An affair based on deception will have a weak foundation, and you'll be too nervous covering your tracks to really enjoy yourself.

Here are a few typical "lines" which have proved successful often enough to be considered priority approaches. Note that not all lines are verbal, but rely more on situations demanding a response from the targeted female.

On a crowded bus:
You step on her foot.
SHE: Owww!
YOU: Oh, I'm dreadfully sorry!
You step on her foot again.
SHE: Ouch! *Please!*
YOU (blushing): Oh, excuse me, please forgive me. I'm not normally so clumsy. It's just that it takes a while for me to get my land legs after I've been out on the yacht.
SHE (wide-eyed): You have a *yacht?*
YOU: Why, do you like boating? . . .
Remember, you don't actually say *you* have a yacht. Later, when she tries to pin you down, you can always say your friend Ari owns the yacht—and he's on a round-the-world voyage. But you offer to take her on a one-week cruise instead.

On a crowded sidewalk:
YOU (arms outstretched in greeting): Mary O'Malley, it's *you!* Three years, three long years! You're lovelier than ever . . .
This one is so old and obvious that it has become credible. Act very confused and flustered when

she denies that she's Mary O'Malley. But be sure to ask, "Well, if you aren't Mary O'Malley, who *are* you?"

In the museum:

Stare at bizarre abstract for five minutes.

YOU: I don't know much about art, but I know what I like.

SHE: I don't think I understand it.

YOU: Me neither.

Awkward silence. Move on to grotesque bust and repeat. After an hour of sharing your befuddlement with her—

YOU: I do better at the zoo. I understand the zoo pretty well.

SHE: Oh, do you like the zoo, too?

YOU: I love it. The children's zoo is just a short walk from here, you know. (Shyly) Would you like to go over?

SHE: That sounds like *real* fun . . .

If your local zoo has a monkey island, take her there. Monkeys do scandalous things in public.

In the supermarket:

YOU: Excuse me, do you know where I can find the frozen raccoon?

SHE (startled): The *what?*

YOU: Frozen raccoon. It's one of those Swanson TV dinners.

SHE: Oh, come on—

YOU: I was skeptical too—(laughing)—but a guy at the record company where I work . . .

This one demands a winning personality. Its strong points are its outrageousness, humor, and obviousness as a pickup. Observe, as in the first example, the technique of identifying yourself immediately by occupation, interests, or income level. In a matter of seconds you can establish yourself as a fascinating, eligible bachelor.

In the museum #2:

Stare at bizarre abstract for five minutes, then nod in judgment, poking cheek with tongue.

YOU: My five-year-old brother has a better notion of line and perspective.

SHE (eyebrows raised): Better than Klee?

YOU: You don't believe me? Look! (Pull folded charcoal line drawing of city skyline from your coat pocket.) Have you ever seen such a display of sweeping vision in conjunction with a draftsman's precision . . .

This line may be a bit shaky unless your kid brother is in the same league with Klee. But maybe not, because she probably knows nothing about art. After all, *Cosmopolitan* sent her to the museum to look for men, not for culture.

In line at the ticket office:

YOU: Excuse me, I don't mean to be forward, but didn't you used to be the receptionist on the 13th floor of the MGM building?

SHE: No, I'm afraid you're mistaken.

YOU: I'm very sorry. (Moment of silence.) Actually, I guess she had brown hair. And she didn't have your figure . . .

SHE: Isn't this a pretty old line?

YOU: What do you take me for, a common masher?

SHE: What do you expect me to take you for with a line like that?

YOU: Listen, I read in *The Sensuous Man* . . .

This approach will work only with a very sophisticated and literate woman. Note also that this line serves two functions—it introduces you and it gets your first argument out of the way at the same time.

In the park:

You fall down on the grass, choking, thrashing your legs, gripping your throat as if you have swallowed your tongue.

SHE (running up): Good heavens! What's happened? What's wrong?

YOU (sitting up, gasping): I think it's better now.

SHE: Can I get you anything?

YOU (shaking head): No, no—I'll be all right. A piece of hot dog went down my windpipe.

SHE: How awful!

YOU: Ohhh—(Breathe deeply.) That's better.

SHE: Are you sure you're all right?

YOU: Oh, yes, I'm fine—I think. You know, it was very courageous of you to approach a strange man choking to death in the park.

SHE (blushing): Oh, not really—

YOU: Yes, really. (Standing and brushing grass off clothes.) In these times of apathy and noninvolvement, it isn't often that one finds a Good Samaritan . . .

This is a very theatrical nonverbal line. It is advisable to dress fairly elegantly when trying this ploy. Few women will approach a shabbily dressed man writhing around on the ground in the park. And a dog on a leash might establish for your would-be rescuer that you are a man of warmth and have roots in the area. (Take a medium-sized, soulful, pathetic dog. A large one may attack either you or your pickup, and an affectionate one may lick you to death before you can pull off your charade.) Above all, make sure there are no policemen or doctors lurking behind nearby bushes. You don't want to have your stomach pumped.

In front of an apartment building:
You puzzle over a dirty scrap of paper in your hands, staring up at street numbers.

YOU (blushing): Pardon me, but do you know where I can find 1523 West Arcane?

SHE: 1523? I don't think there is a 1523—this is 1521, and next is 1525—

YOU: Maybe it's 1523 *East* Arcane—

SHE: Sure, that must be—

YOU: No, beyond Walnut, East Arcane turns into East Partridge Row, so it must be *West* Arcane.

SHE: It might be West *Acorn*, do you think?

YOU: No, I distinctly remember him saying it was *Arcane*. Maybe the number is wrong! Does this look like a one or a three? (Show her the scrap of paper.) It's smudged rather badly—

SHE: Oh, I think it's a one. The writing is

kind of jerky, like it was written on the bus—

YOU: Then it must be 1521. That's *your* building, then. Do you know Roger Endive?

SHE: No, I don't think anybody by that name lives in my building . . .

Conversations of this sort can carry on for so long that they provide enough momentum for a personal introduction. And even if you don't get anywhere in that single approach, you can pop in and out of the neighborhood, waving pleasant hellos from across the street, until you have become a familiar face and another opportunity arises to get on a firmer footing with your target.

On a crowded sidewalk:

You cut the corner too sharply and knock fourteen gift-wrapped packages out of her arms and across the sidewalk.

YOU: Oh my goodness, excuse me! I'm dreadfully sorry—

SHE (wearily): That's all right—if you could just—

YOU: Of course! (Lunging back and forth across sidewalk, picking up packages.)

> Here! Here! Here's another! No, no, let me get that—(You slip *your* little package into the pile in her arms—the 49¢ gift you carry around with you in a box with a ribbon [and your business card]. Then you tip your hat and beat a hasty retreat.) So sorry—

If she is honest, she will have to call the number on your card to return your package. You, of course, will express immense gratitude that the gift has been found, and will offer to rush right over to her place to pick it up. And, once you have it in your possession, you will further express your thanks in the form of an invitation to the theater, to dinner, or to whatever you think you can get away with.

As each of these lines demonstrates, it isn't so much *what* you do or say that matters, but *how*. A really smooth operator can pick up a girl while speaking a foreign language. This talent is largely a reflection of confidence and superficial charm. If you've got it, by all means, use it.

But if you don't have it—the sort of personality that wins women over in seconds—then the public arena is not really your place to meet women. You require more intimate and natural contact with a woman for your good qualities to emerge.

Do not despair. Your requirements can be met.

7.

The Search for the Ideal Woman

You aren't looking for just any woman, you know. You're looking for a certain type of woman that turns you on—physically, emotionally, and/or intellectually. So the first thing to do is to draw up some sort of mental image of your ideal mate. Be realistic, though. Don't conjure up a film goddess or a mythical supervirgin on a pedestal. And, while you're at it, figure out what sort of woman is likely to go for *you*. This calls for some honest and critical self-evaluation, but if you really know who you are you will have a better chance of finding your female counterpart.

For example, try to "type-cast" yourself. Could you describe yourself as a he-man type or a jock? Are you a brain? Do you see yourself as a party-goer or one of the "beautiful people"? Are you an outdoorsman? Are you a steady, conservative breadwinner? Are you a banker, insurance man, or country-club type? Are you an "easy-come, easy-go" type, dancing through life without a care? Are you a father figure? Are you a poet or some other deep emotional type? Are you a romantic? Or a politician? A martyr? A laborer?

Whatever type of person you are, there are plenty of women looking for just that sort. Many women crave the comfort, security, and respectability that you, as, say, a successful insurance broker, can offer. And they'll pick you over that flashy, charming, but erratic and irresponsible sex-book writer every time. And don't feel that you're at a disadvantage in competing with that muscular mountain of football player you went to school with. Maybe the cheerleaders swooned over him (they go for that type), but most of the girls in your class thought he was a vain, insensitive, muscle-headed lummox.

Every woman is looking for something different in a man. Some are suckers for intellect, some for tenderness, some for household skills, some for piety, some for wit, some for steadfastness, some for companionship, some for creativity, and some—too many—for money.

But here's the problem. Many men have occupations or travel in circles which do not coincide with their real types (too many poets are selling typewriters). And they don't often meet the sort of females who will respond to their particular chemistry. I've had that problem. For much of my adult life I have lived in a performer's world, surrounded by beautiful, extroverted actresses. Unfortunately, I am by nature a more down-to-earth, inward-looking sort. And I would sooner converse with a baboon than with the average starlet.

But the lack of attractive prospects in my professional life has not held me back. I happen to be a music lover, so I go girl-hunting at concerts and music festivals—not among the performers, but in the *audience*. It figures that a woman who is moved by music that moves me will be on somewhat the same wavelength as mine. And such is usually the case.

So think! What is really important in your life? Politics? Then you might hit it off with a woman who shares your electoral passions, perhaps one you meet in the campaign organization of a local candidate. Are you caught up in your own psyche? Then join a therapy group or an encounter session. Are you religious? Sign up for a church group. Are you a lover of Christmas music? Then join a Salvation Army band—you may meet *the* woman and get married after a decent engagement of, say, twelve years.

The good thing about joining some sort of organization to meet women is that you don't need to know anybody, you will meet women who share your interests and outlook, you will get to know each other without the awkwardness that accompanies a pickup or a blind date, and you can drop out if it doesn't work.

The bad thing about joining such a group is that you may have to pay dues, attend meetings, and labor for many hours just to look over a few prospects who may not pan out. You may run into women who are *too much* like you (you don't want a carbon copy of yourself—a woman should have some freshness and mystery to her). You may turn into a compulsive "joiner." Or you might unknowingly end up as a member of a Communist-front group and have your phone tapped by the FBI (you might even be dating an *agent* of the FBI!).

If you can, get involved in an activity that you will find fulfilling even if you don't meet any attractive and potentially bedable women. Taking a course in a community college, while a fine way of flushing out intelligent single women, is worthwhile in itself. And you might look into a "free university" if there is one in your area. Most free universities offer courses that are inexpensive, informal, and meet in the homes of teachers or students. The party atmosphere of such classes lends itself to intimate involvement with attractive female students (don't be fooled by stereotypes—some free universities cater only to radicals and weirdos, but not all). I would advise caution, however. The course which is advertised as an "encounter session" may turn out to be a nude "group-grope" with strangers. And I mean *strange*-ers.

Meanwhile, keep looking for women at parties. If you're a wit, a storyteller, or a poet, take in all the cocktail parties. If you're a sports buff, attend the social gatherings at the country club and fascinate everybody with your account of the final round of the 1956 Open. If you're light on your feet, go to as many dances as you can stand—and keep changing partners. Best of all, of course, is the informal get-together at a friend's house. You can meet women there in an atmosphere free of "dating pressure."

Finally, you can rely on your friends to be matchmakers. This can be dangerous because your friends may *think* they know a girl who is just perfect for you and, Oh God, it's Elsa Lanchester in *Bride of Frankenstein.* On the other hand, doesn't it follow that, if your friends like this girl, she must have something going for her? What have you got to lose besides a few hours, your dignity, and your friends? You may finally hit on a real gem of a girl—the kind who is beautiful, charming, intelligent, warm, sexy, and fucks like a rabbit. So don't turn your back on your helpful friends unless they have fully demonstrated their incompetence as matchmakers.

I would, however, avoid the *blind date* unless you've got a strong stomach and a high tolerance for boredom. Maybe I've been unlucky—after all, I've heard hundreds of stories about blind dates who hit it off and later married, living happily ever after—but I have never gone on a blind date without getting burned. The most memorable of my blind dates include:

1. A 170-pound female track star who kept pinching my biceps and guessing my time in the 440-yard dash.
2. A very pretty college girl who said her grandfather was the original Roto-Rooter man, and taught me all I know about drains, pipes, and cesspools.
3. A pious coed who slapped me and called me an "Antichrist" for something I said about an early Pope.
4. A girl who chewed an entire pack of gum at once.
5. A woman (one of those incessant talkers) who spent the whole date describing her ideal man—who was absolutely nothing like me—and denouncing the average male as a sex-maddened animal.

Blind dates, I have concluded, are blind for a reason. And usually a *good* reason. So, when my friends want to introduce me to an eligible female, I have them arrange a little party at their home. They invite her. They invite me. And, if the magic isn't there, nothing is lost—we still have our friends to talk to.

Figure the percentages, then. If you join all the clubs, take night courses, go to plays and concerts, attend every party, and meet every woman your friends throw in the ring, you're *bound* to meet a few who approximate your specifications. And, once you have a woman in your sights, go back and reread this book; take her some place romantic; and then unleash all your newfound sensuality.

You'll be incredible. Christ, I bet you won't even recognize yourself.

8.

How to Drive a Woman to Ecstasy

Assuming you have found your ideal woman—or at least a woman who will do until *that* one comes along—it's time you learned how to make love to her so capably that your mutual satisfaction, your outright *ecstasy,* is assured.

Half of sex is simply "you"—your personality, your ethics, your attitudes toward women and your body. The other half, the half without which all this personality and involvement mean nothing, is your sexual *skill.* We can break the notion of "skill" down still further into the following elements:

1. Sexual knowledge—awareness of *where* a woman's body is most responsive; and what techniques and positions may be employed to elicit that response.
2. Physical ability—the capability of *using* your body and employing these myriad techniques to achieve mutual fulfillment.

These are the matters which are discussed in this chapter, the *gut* of sex—"How to Do It." Your task is obvious and straightforward. By reading this chapter you will obtain "knowledge." And by practicing these techniques you will develop your "physical ability."

The end result, the blending of these two elements, will be sexual *skill.* And one hell of a good time.

Female Erogenous Zones

Most men think there are two areas of a woman's body that are sexually responsive—the breasts and the vagina. They're not wrong, but they're not right either. Practically every square inch of the female body has the ability to become fully erotic, and no man can consider himself a great lover until he has learned to explore and take pleasure in *all* of his woman's sexual potential. To accomplish this, there are two techniques you must master: the dexterous use of your hands, and the kiss. Sensuality Exercises Numbers 9 and 10 have helped you improve your sense of touch, and Exercise Number 8 plus the sensitivity instructions given in this chapter should make you a Sensuous Man.

Now let's take a look at your girl's body.

THE EYES

Butterfly kisses (eyelashes to eyelashes) are fun. Run your lips across her eyelids softly as if she were being touched by butterfly wings. (If her soft, feathery lashes are improbably long, be careful not to dislodge them. Modern technology leaves no stone unturned these days, and the most gorgeous lashes are usually false.)

Many women love to see pornographic erotica (though few will admit it) in the form of novels, illustrations, photographs, and blue movies. Display your collection (if you own one) where she can notice it, and be guided by whether or not she shows any interest.

THE NOSE

The clean fresh smell of a new-bathed man is great, but to help today's lovers even more there are subtle, sexy colognes to turn a gal on. Spend an extra buck here for good imported toilet waters. The cheap stuff smells awful. Place the cologne strategically, but not too heavily, on the face and neck, on the chest and lower abdomen, and on the backs of your hands.

THE EARS

You're now approaching one of the most highly erotic zones of the lady's body. The ear lobes are particularly sensitive to the flick and kiss of your tongue. The combined techniques of lobe-nibbling and directed breathing on the ears can transform a rather unresponsive woman into a willing partner. When blowing into a woman's ear, don't use force enough to stun her. Rather, exhale a soft, warm breath in and around her ear in conjunction with your nibbling and tongueing of her ear. Many women have ears so sensitive that the merest contact will cause them to shiver in excitation. Don't be sloppy and wet her entire ear, and remember to do and say everything softly when you're that close.

THE MOUTH

The mouth is the most beautiful, the most sensitive, the most active organ you can reach while she's still dressed. The kiss is probably the single most important move toward the bedroom. It's the key! It turns her on—or off—and, since life is a lot better when you turn her on, you can hardly do too much homework in this lesson of love.

1. *Don't* crush her lips against her teeth to show your passion.
2. *Don't* squeeze the breath out of her as you're kissing her.
3. *Don't* try to ram your tongue down her throat in order to stimulate her.
4. *Don't* bite her lips.
5. *Don't* use a dry, birdlike, pecking kiss with no pressure at all.
6. *Don't* kiss with your mouth wide open and slobber all over her.
7. *Don't* drool as you kiss her.
8. *Don't* hold a kiss so long she can't breathe.
9. *Don't, don't, don't* have bad breath.

Now that you know why you've been a lonesome lover all these years, let's get to the good part.

1. *Do* cushion your lips against hers rather than pressing. This will keep your front teeth cov-

ered and avoid any initial hard contact which may offend her.

2. *Do* let your tongue just touch the area inside her lips as you brush across them, but don't penetrate beyond her teeth at this point.
3. *Do* begin raising her sexual temperature with sensitive, probing kisses, then
4. *Do* proceed more boldly once you have established that she is enjoying your kisses.
5. *Do* let your tongue slip between her teeth until you touch her tongue. Withdraw and see if she follows you. Repeat this tactic until she is following your tongue as quickly as you are inserting and withdrawing it.
6. *Do* switch occasionally to nipping (not biting) her lower lip and sucking it in slightly between your lips. Vary the area coverage . . . kiss her ear lobes again, . . . her eyes, . . . her neck. (I particularly like the pulsating spot where the ear, the neck, and the jawline all come together.)
7. *Do* keep your tongue narrow and pointed, not broad and flat. Your tongue is larger than hers, and filling up her mouth with it may give her a panicky feeling.
8. *Do* notice any shyness about, or rejection of, your soul kiss. If there is, retreat from penetrating so deeply into her mouth. Start again slowly until you feel she is accepting and welcoming your tongue action once more.

9. *Do* kiss her again and again and again and again. Kissing is the first beautiful, intimate contact between a man and a woman, a preliminary quickening of each other's senses and sensuality.

THE BREASTS

From the beginning of time, men have looked at, measured, painted, sculpted, photographed, and worshiped women's breasts. We suck them from the day we are born, and are drawn to them for the rest of our lives. Breasts are beautiful, and we never let women forget it. Before you take the "whole world in your hands" though, let's discuss these lovely ornaments.

Women are as hung up about the size and shape of their breasts as men are about their cocks. Unlike penises, however, female breast sensations can vary. Some breasts are completely incapable of sensation, while some are so responsive that stimulation can create clitoral orgasm. There are cases on record of women having frequent orgasms while nursing their babies. (Makes you wonder how those kids ever got weaned, doesn't it?) Despite these massive individual differences, women are unanimous on one point: They don't like for their breasts to be handled roughly. It seems that a depressing number of men are breast grabbers, squeezers, and biters. Women have as much fear of being injured in the breasts as you have of being kicked in the balls, so use your head and proceed gently and slowly when you do your breast work.

One of the most effective methods of arousing the female is to stroke the breasts in a soothing manner, brushing your hands and fingers softly and slowly over the nipples. Then cup one nipple in the palm of your hand and move the hand in a lazy, clockwise motion, 'round and 'round, until the friction creates the beginning of nipple erection.

Now you can commence fondling the breasts more firmly while you maneuver a nipple between your lips (see Sensuality Exercise Number 8). Alternate kneading and licking actions on one breast while you are titillating the other nipple with your thumb and index finger. Kiss and suck, kiss and suck the nipples, run the tongue around the entire nipple area, the aureola (the dark area around the nipple). Hold both breasts in your hands, bring the nipples together, and run your tongue across them in a rapid, flicking motion. Your hands should be gentle, your mouth soft, and your tongue a wildly darting stimulant to these most prized and delicious erogenous zones.

Special care should be taken during and before menstruation, when the breasts are slightly enlarged and more likely to be ultrasensitive to strong stroking or sucking. Some women's breasts are so tender at this time of the month that they can't stand caressing at all.

To be sure that you don't cause her discomfort that she's too polite to express to you, ask her directly some night about what times of the month her breasts are most capable of sexual sensation, if they hurt during menstruation, and for how long.

There are times, during the height of passion particularly, when you can handle her breasts a bit more firmly. Not roughly—*firmly*. Slightly pinching the nipples at this point can be a welcome and lusty sexual by-play, but use good common sense. While a slight momentary pinch can be joyous, too much pressure will hurt her and detract from the love-making mood.

THE CLITORIS

The man who knows how to caress a woman's clitoris will never lack ardent bedmates. You can't consider yourself a good lover until you can wring orgasms from her clitoris with the artistry that a great violinist displays in extracting exquisite music from his violin.

The clitoris is the female equivalent of the penis. It comes in different sizes, becomes erect when sexually stimulated, and is the seat of orgasm. Unlike the penis, however, the clitoris often retracts and even seems to disappear during the plateau and orgasmic phases (imagine, if you can, your penis reversing itself and being swallowed up by your body), it does not ejaculate, usually responds more slowly to sexual stimulation, and has a much, much lower pain threshold than your cock.

Judging from what women have told me, the deplorable truth is that at least 75 percent of American men don't know how to caress the clitoris. Here are some common mistakes:

1. *Don't* employ direct manipulation on the clitoris in the early stages.
2. *Don't* stop exciting her manually (or orally) if you lose contact with the clitoris.
3. *Don't* stop stimulation at the point of orgasm.
4. *Don't* use the same tactile stimulation pattern for any length of time.
5. *Don't* assume that she is "all through" after having just one orgasm.

Being guilty of even one of these *don'ts* is robbing her of sexual pleasure. If you're guilty of all of them, you ought to be robbed of *your* sexual pleasure.

In my backward, pre-sensuous days, I used to think that when I stuck my hand down a girl's panties and pushed her clitoris back and forth with my fingers a few times, I was giving her a big thrill. I was really showing my ignorance of one of the most crucial parts of her anatomy.

Always begin with indirect manipulation of the clitoris. I caress the mons area first and then move on, after she is obviously responding, to the right and then the left side of the clitoral shaft and then back again to the mons area. It's vital to vary techniques, as concentration on one area with a single technique can cause numbness, and nothing is more disheartening than a numb clitoris. Avoid direct stimulation of the tip of the clitoris until just before orgasm (hers, not yours, you fool!), and be sparing and gentle to avoid the possibility of causing pain. Some women can't stand direct contact even then, so check this out thoroughly with her before leaping in with heavy fingers.

I always make sure that the clitoris remains

lubricated by using (1) the juices from her vagina, (2) my saliva, or (3) an antiseptic jelly or cream such as K-Y jelly, vaseline, or one of the many others on the market. If you don't keep her clitoris moist, those pleasurable sensations you're creating will quickly turn to pain.

One of the dumbest mistakes men make is to stop manipulation when the woman reaches orgasm. *Women desire and need continued stimulation during orgasm,* so keep those fingers busy.

Many a man has had the experience of lying there, happily exciting her clitoris, and finding himself suddenly unable to find the damn thing. Don't start feeling around for it, just keep on manipulating the mons area and clitoral shaft, and she will continue to respond and will reach orgasm shortly thereafter. Retraction of the clitoris during advanced excitation is normal, and your failure to continue stimulation will create strong frustration in the highly excited female and cause her to lose her orgasmic ability temporarily—something that will not exactly endear you to her.

After she has had that orgasm, wait a minute or two (as the clitoris will be extremely sensitive to the touch immediately after climax) and then bring her to orgasm again. Most women need at least three automanipulative orgasms before they are satisfied. But don't worry. Your fingers aren't going to be worn down to the nub. After you've warmed her up with the first orgasm, the others can be attained relatively quickly.

THE VAGINA

The altar at which we all worship. From the day we come out, we connive, cajole, compliment, and buy our way back in. Men have lost fortunes, kings have abdicated, brothers have betrayed brothers, and governments have toppled—all because of this little cavern of joy we happily call pussy, cunt, twat, quim, box, hole—and Heaven.

One of the most harmful myths that have been perpetrated on the female in the last few years is that there is only one kind of orgasm that counts—the vaginal orgasm. In point of fact, there is no such thing. All female orgasms are clitoral in origin. You can keep your cock in her vagina for the next ten years (well, maybe *you* can) but, unless you directly or indirectly stimulate her clitoris, she isn't going to have an orgasm. That doesn't mean though that the vagina isn't an important seat of erotic feeling, because it is. The first point is psychological. When you enter a woman she feels possessed—a necessary factor to her sexual well-being.

Physically, women consider their vaginas to be their primary sexual instrument. A woman reasons thus, of course, because it is here that she receives the male. It is also here that the male has an unfailing clue to how effectively he has been able to arouse her, for the female achieves lubrication within ten to thirty seconds after you have initiated effective sexual stimulation. Until your woman has become moist and juicy, you cannot enter her—unless you want to be called a selfish bastard.

As the woman becomes more excited, the inner two-thirds of the vagina lengthens and becomes distended—ready to accept any size cock she's likely to encounter. To test for lubrication, insert one or two fingers in the vagina. If she is wet inside, you may now excite her further by simulating the in-and-out motion of the penis with your fingers. Pay particular attention to the upper part of the vagina near the entrance, so you can indirectly stimulate the clitoris as well.

Now that you have her vagina completely lubricated, it is time to proceed to . . .

Putting It In—and Out—and In—Etc.

When it comes to sexual positions, I'm a pretty simple guy. I've had my years of acrobatic maneuvers designed to strain every ligament and nerve in my body and have settled down to *comfortable* fucking. If you want to make love standing on your head, in a backward arch with both feet and hands on the floor, or balancing on one foot, go ahead. But don't expect me to work up any enthusiasm over the possibility of a sprained back, bruised body, and fractured skull. There's enough for two people to do to each other in love-making to keep you both busy for a lifetime without going out looking for positions that are pure hospital bait. That doesn't mean you shouldn't be imaginative—just forgo foolhardy ventures unless you're a trained aerialist.

The classic positions have a lot to offer: They have already been tested and proved able to create maximum pleasure, variety, and the opportunity to shine performancewise no matter what physique you're staggering around with.

Basically, there are two general sets of positions: lying down and sitting up. Let's start out with that prone classic:

THE MISSIONARY POSITION

She lies flat on her back, legs spread apart. You stretch out on top of her, face to face, your weight supported by your arms, slightly flexed knees, and feet. (You see how proficiency at push-ups pays off here?)

The Missionary Position supposedly gets its name from an episode that occurred in the South Sea islands. One day a group of natives (who were accustomed to practicing rear-entry intercourse only) were spying on a missionary and his wife while they were making love and the natives became highly amused at the view of the couple engaged in face-to-face intercourse. The word quickly spread around the island about that crazy Western practice, and it was nicknamed The Missionary by the natives. It is also known in America as the Male-Dominant position, and it is probably the most popular of all positions.

A resourceful lover can employ uncounted variations of the Missionary Position and achieve very rewarding sensations. Her legs can be lifted to rest on your shoulders, or locked around your waist. Slip a pillow beneath the buttocks for deeper penetration. Lift yourself high in the "saddle" to achieve strong clitoral reaction. At the moment of truth, reach down and cup her buttocks in both your hands.

THE FLOATER

This is the reverse of the Missionary: The man lies on the bottom, the woman on top, prone. The male uses his pelvic muscles to thrust his penis in and out while she "floats" on top doing relatively little work. Sensuality Exercise Number 4 put you in condition for this one, remember.

THE "ROLL ME OVER, DO IT AGAIN"

She lies on her back, you enter, and then, holding on to each other closely to avoid allowing your penis to fall out of her vagina, you roll over on your side, carrying her with you. Once in place, you can continue penile thrusts.

THE EASY RIDER

You're on the bottom again. She sits on top of you, drawing her legs up in front of her. This time you're the "floater" and she does all the work, raising and lowering her body to allow the penis to go in and out, in and out. To vary the position, your girl can lean forward across your chest, resting her weight on her elbows, or she can lean backward and brace her hands against the bed for support.

I particularly like this position, as it affords me great control and gives me a stimulating view of all my favorite things. I can hold her head in my hands and bring her lips down to mine. I can cup her breasts or race past her belly button to her clitoris.

THE SEE-SAW

You sit facing each other, legs apart and stretched out (hers over your thighs). You hold each other first by the shoulders, then slowly let yourselves fall backward just enough so that you are now holding each other by your outstretched hands. Now rock back and forth. This is silly, but fun, as much of sex play should be. The laughter and light in her eyes show she's happy. The magnificent tumescence of your prick, ditto.

THE UNEMPLOYMENT COMPENSATION

You sit facing each other, as in the See-Saw . . . and sit and sit and sit with your cock in her cunt for an hour or so—meditating, talking, contemplating each other's navel, caressing, and now and then indulging in enough thrusts to maintain your erection. When you can't stand waiting another hour, you progress to the usual orgasmic pleasures. It's an old East Indian custom which is ideally suited to the luxurious leisure of the unemployed. Since I've never been fully unemployed, I've not tried this one, but I'm told that certain personality types find it a lot of fun.

THE LASSIE

She kneels and bends forward, resting her elbows across a couch or hassock. You stand behind her. Have her raise her buttocks as high as possible and then put your penis into her vagina. Your two hands are free and can now be used to excite her breasts and clitoris as you go —right—you guessed it: in and out of her vagina. The greatest depth of penetration is effected utilizing this position. There is also an unmatched feeling of power as you hold her hips tightly against your groin, her body helpless to resist your powerful thrusts.

THE SLIDING POND

Put your girl in a soft, upholstered chair and kneel in front of her so your head comes about to the level of her breasts. Your knees should just touch the bottom of the chair . . . and you should have a hell of a hard-on.

Now slide her off the chair and right onto that beautiful erect shaft. The feeling is dizzying. She is wet and very, very hot; you are face to face and in about as deep as you can be. Lean her back. The chair will support her. She can now rest her feet on the floor and her elbows on the chair, and she'll have good hip mobility. You lean back with your hands on the floor and raise your pelvis to plunge into her for a few moments, and then she should take over the action by moving her pelvic area up and down on your penis—faster and faster. The Sliding Pond is an exciting way to come. When you do explode, you'll find yourself in each other's arms—exhausted, wet, beautiful—a total state of A.F.O.—all fucked out.

There are, of course, dozens of variations on each of the positions described here. Sex is so highly personalized that what turns me on could leave you cold and vice versa. That's why I continue to experiment. Making love should be like embarking on a great adventure, destination known, itinerary subject to whim and fancy.

Nibbling, Nipping, Eating, Licking, and Sucking

If I were marooned on a desert island and could have only one girl and five books with me, it would take me a while to choose the girl, but the books I could pick instantly: *Tom Jones*, an anthology of Damon Runyon's stories, *Better Homes and Gardens' Family Medical Guide*, *The Complete Works of Shakespeare*, and *An Encylopaedic Outline of Oral Technique in Genital Excitation*. Gershon Legman, the author of the last-named work, estimates that there are at least 14,288,400 potentially lively ways of making oral love, and I intend to try every one of his suggestions (not that I'm hoping to be dumped on an island to rack up a score).

There are still a few refugees from the *Mayflower* walking around who think going down on a woman or sucking her breasts is dirty or perverted. Even if their wives sprayed themselves with Lysol disinfectant, these men wouldn't think their women's genitals were clean enough for their lips and tongues to touch.

You can't do much about men who divide love-making into columns marked "right" and "wrong" but feel sorry for them and hope they'll eventually seek professional counsel or get a brain transplant.

I've been tasting the hot, moist, fragrant love juices from women's pussies for much of my lifetime, marveling at the variety of bouquets and flavors that emanate from this never-ending fountain.

Since all Sensuous Men are ardent and proficient at nibbling, nipping, eating, licking, and sucking, there's no point in your trying to fake a broken tongue or charley horse of the lower lip as an excuse to skip out on oral sex. *You're going to have to learn oral skills* if you want female admiration and a niche in the Great Lovers' Hall of Fame. A negative attitude won't even rate you a signed tongue-print in the outer corner of the parking lot.

GENERAL ORAL TECHNIQUES

Think of your tongue as a hot electric wire causing a slight shock sensation wherever it touches. Run it over her ear lobes, neck, mouth, nose, and eyes. Dwell on her nipples and breasts, swirling and sucking as you go. Slide your tongue like a tiny paintbrush along the small of her back, the sides of her waist, and the insides of her legs. Lick behind her knees and kiss the tops of her feet. Then wend your way to the fuse—the clitoris. Go near it, around it, over it, and along it, continuing soft licking and gentle sucking until she reaches orgasm.

Now you are ready for a few more-advanced techniques.

THE ALTERNATING FLAME

This is really fiery. Cunnilingus at its teasing best. Start at her knees. Kiss the inside of her leg very lingeringly, then alternate to the other leg. Proceed upward slowly in this manner, kissing first one and then the other thigh until you reach that phantasmagoric area—the cunt—and dip your tongue into what should now be a bubbling volcano.

THE STRAWBERRY SUCKLE

Sprinkle the breasts with soft kisses and then follow up with nibbling of the aureola (dark circle around the nipple). Now, slip your tongue over the same area, circling the nipple faster, faster, faster (as if you were running around and around in a revolving door). Next, draw the nipple into your mouth, knead it gently, and then begin sucking, pulling as much of the breast into your mouth as you can, pressing it firmly between the tongue and roof of your mouth. Suck as a baby does while being fed. Repeat all steps many times, alternating from breast to breast.

THE RUNAWAY PINCH

This one is a quickie in the truest sense. Take the tips of your thumb and index finger and bring them together as if they were a pair of foam-rubber tweezers: open, shut, open, shut. Then, using this gentle tweezing action, begin *very lightly* and *quickly* pinching her behind, thighs, stomach, nipples, arms, legs—everywhere you can reach. Be sure to move your fingers like streaked lightning, or you won't produce the desired effect.

The Runaway Pinch can also be done with your mouth. Just be sure to stretch your lips until they cover the sharp edges of your teeth to avoid inadvertently nicking or cutting her soft skin.

THE UPSIDE-DOWN KISS

Walk her around to the back of an upholstered chair. Sit her atop the back and, holding onto her hands, lower her gently onto the seat of the chair. Are you following? If you're on target, the back of her head and her shoulders are now resting on the seat of the chair, while her rear end is just near the top of the chair-back and her legs are resting on your shoulders. Simply lean down and kiss that whole wonderful wide, wide world of love.

THE FEATHERY FLICK

Raise her right through the roof with this one. Locate that fascinating clitoris—the most sensitive little sex organ in her body—with your tongue. Flick the tip of your tongue back and forth along the top of the shaft, in much the same way you would stroke a banjo but, of course, with a much lighter touch. Now flick up into the mons area, back down again along the clitoral shaft, and *finally*, when she is very excited, move your tongue down to the tip of the clitoris and continue with a feathery flick until she comes.

THE VELVET BUZZ SAW

Stiffen your tongue, place it at the tip of her shaft, and move your head from left to right as though you are saying no—but do it rapidly so that your tongue is brushing her clitoris—a dozen times a second.

The Velvet Buzz Saw is particularly effective with women who have trouble achieving orgasm and women who need a number of orgasms to reach satiation. Be sure, however, that you've excited your woman sufficiently beforehand, as the clitoris is too sensitive for the Velvet Buzz Saw until it has been stimulated with gentler techniques.

"69"

One of the best oral-genital positions for mutual satisfaction. Lie atop or alongside the woman with your head toward her feet, and vice versa. As you kiss and suck her clitoral region, she is able to take your penis into her mouth and caress your balls. Should you both desire, you may come to orgasm in this popular position.

THE AFTER-KISS

After intercourse, when you open your eyes and look at each other, kiss her softly—on the lips, on the eyes, on the nose, on the hollow of her neck, and then back up to her lips again. You're silently telling her she is a Sensuous Woman and that you enjoyed her. This after-kiss, as I call it, can be as important as the initial kiss—

if there is to be a next time.

Anal Sex

The Good Housekeeping Seal of Approval isn't being given out this year to ass-fuckers. But don't let that slow you down. Being unconventional has its own rewards.

Since most women are afraid of anal sex,

think it's perverted, and (if they've thought it through that far) a source of vaginal infection, you'll need to exercise great patience and consideration in persuading her to try it "just this once."

Be sensitive to the right moment. Use your tongue to begin the first step to anal intercourse. There's almost no fecal matter in the colon until the moment of defecation so, after she is bathed and perfumed, run your tongue across her back and up her thighs. Spread her cheeks, and wet the anus with your tongue. She may be quite tense at first but, if you massage the anal area with well-lubricated fingers (antiseptic jelly or Vaseline is useful), she should start to relax.

Now insert one finger in the anus and rotate it from side to side. Gently rotating your finger will contribute to her sense of relaxation and soon will generate warm, positive feelings. Use more lubricant and insert your finger again, penetrating deeper into the anus each time. Withdraw and insert. Withdraw and insert.

Be extremely sensitive to her reactions to avoid causing her stress or pain.

Lubricate your penis from top to bottom, using an extra generous amount of cream on and around the head.

Now place the head of the penis up against

the anal opening. Permit her to push back against you so she can control the initial slow entrance. When the head of the penis penetrates the rectum, hold still for a moment to allow her sphincter muscle to adjust to the newcomer.

You may now proceed—with care—as you do in normal intercourse, thrusting in and out.

If you can simultaneously play with her clitoris (make sure your hands are clean), chances are that she will have a most satisfying orgasm as she experiences this new sensation.

And one comforting plus-factor for you in anal intercourse is that you can ejaculate into the anus without any possibility of impregnating the lady.

Anal sex is an exhilarating part of the fun and games two people play with each other's bodies in the never-ending desire to explore and experience, but it carries certain risks.

1. If your girl has a real hang-up about it, she will probably not enjoy it.
2. Unless both partners have carefully bathed and thoroughly deodorized, the experience may not be aesthetically pleasing.
3. Long or jagged fingernails can do dreadful damage and will disqualify you from this game immediately.

4. If you don't proceed with extreme care and caution, anal sex can be painful.
5. Vaginismus is a hazard, unless you make sure that neither your hands nor penis touch the vaginal area before a thorough washing with soap and warm water.

Follow these instructions carefully, and you and your lady will enjoy a completely new sensation in love-making. Unless, of course, you've taken up with one of the *Good Housekeeping* ladies—in which case you may be forced to go back to holding hands.

Sexual Ethics

Ethics are a very personal thing, yet I consider them the most important part of a man's character. They set the tone for his entire life, and he will be judged on that basis by both men and women.

Every man, consciously or not, has a code of ethics. And no two codes are alike. Over the years, I have evolved a sort of code for myself, a few rules that have "worked" for me, meaning that they have contributed to honest and meaningful relationships with women. Since many ethical matters relate to your whole approach as a lover, they are covered in other chapters. But here are a few rules worth isolating at this time. They are not the "law" by any means—you have to answer to your own conscience—but they can serve as a model for your own code of ethics.

Don't Gossip

Sexual intimacy with a woman is beautiful. She is giving you her most precious commodity —herself. But your knowledge of her intimate sexual habits should be strictly privileged information. Her reputation is important to her, and you have no right to jeopardize it by immature bragging in the company of others. Keep your mouth shut.

Sure, other guys do it. There are always one or two men in a group (like my friend Frank from Chapter 2) who go on and on about all the chicks they've made it with. If they're making it all up, no real harm is done. But if they're talking about women you know, then they have violated a confidence (if the story is true) or slandered a good name (if it is false).

Also, don't give much credence to the stories of guys who *do* shoot off their mouths. I have heard enough gossip from the braggarts' female counterparts to know that the loudmouth is usually a liar. My money is on the quiet guy as the most active sex cat. After all, a man who respects women is more likely to succeed with them. Put more simply, the doers don't talk, and the talkers usually don't do.

Protect Her—She'll Love You for It

While sex is equal between a man and a woman, and while she loves it as much as you do, there is one outstanding difference—she can become pregnant. We men *cannot* get pregnant, which is probably why we tend to take the possible consequences of our sexual affairs more lightly than most women. Making babies is the last thing on our minds when we're slipping our hands under a girl's dress on the way home from the movies.

Such an attitude is short-sighted. Women may have to give birth to babies (Women's Lib or no, I don't want to share *that* function), but men are equally responsible for them, both financially and morally. The financial aspect is obvious. Even *not* having a conceived child—

an abortion—is expensive. And actually raising a child, as beautiful as that can be, is a fiscal calamity. As they say in the restaurant business, if you aren't ready to foot the bill, you've got no business looking at the menu. For the married couple, the unwanted child can be a burden which can foster resentment, spoil a marriage, or destroy a career. For the bachelor, even worse—unless he's an irresponsible lout.

Any way you look at it, a pregnancy which is not supported by a shared commitment and responsibility by both partners is a disaster.

Since I am not writing a standard "marriage guide," I will forgo the usual detailed information about contraceptives. Every book on the subject covers this territory thoroughly—condoms, foams, jellies, IUD's, the pill—and I have nothing to add to the routine medical lore. At one time or another my ladies and I have employed every common method of birth control except the rhythm method, and I haven't had an accident yet. The pill, of course, has been the most convenient method, and it seems to be the most reliable.

But I do have several very reasonable and practical comments which relate both to sexual ethics and to your effectiveness and enjoyment as a lover:

If birth control is called for, *be sure.* Not just for the reasons above, but because you can't have good sex if you're worried about getting your bedmate pregnant. And she will not respond well if she suspects that you are using her for your own satisfaction without regard for the consequences.

You might beat the odds by taking a chance, but why risk it?

If, despite your mutual efforts at contraception, your woman gets pregnant; or if the two of you lose your heads at the height of passion and screw without protection, with disastrous results—then face up to it. Both of you are in this mess together.

If you're in love and both of you *want* to get married, then the situation is not so black. Otherwise, this is her most frightened moment. Unwed and pregnant. It is your duty to assume the responsibility. If she wants to have the baby outside of wedlock, you have no right to abandon her or threaten her into a forced abortion. You should offer to assume your fair share of child support.

If she wants the abortion, *you* must find the doctor; you must make sure that he is not a quack; you must pay for the abortion; and you should go with her to protect her and see that she gets home safely afterwards. And you do *not* drop her like a hot potato the instant she reports that the abortion is successful. Follow up the unfortunate incident by being as considerate and helpful as possible. Do anything you can to make it easier for her. She may sink into a deep depression. If so, do what you can to distract her from her troubles and cheer her up.

But you are *not* obligated to take full blame for her pregnancy. That must be shared equally between the two of you. It is unethical on her part to make you feel like a cad if she was as enthusiastic as you when your passions were high.

Leave Married Women Alone

She may be a great lay, but if you're a bachelor I recommend staying away from the married woman. There are plenty of lovely young chicks around who want loving and are available. They can sleep over, go away on weekends, and clean your apartment for you. Furthermore, you don't have to go to out-of-the-way restaurants with the single woman, or skulk around in motels.

Those are the practical advantages of restricting yourself to single girls. The ethical side is more complicated and, in this instance, more ambiguous. I personally don't believe that a single man should inject himself into a married woman's life, because he has little control over the effect his presence may exert on her husband and her children—not to mention the marriage itself. I have little respect for the bachelor who breaks up marriage after marriage by seducing women who are only looking for a little sympathy and excitement.

Even if you're married, I can't wholeheartedly endorse an affair with the married woman. But I can certainly see the good side of such an arrangement. It may be the best and most convenient thing for both of you, and you can always commiserate with each other about the kids.

The wishes of the married woman have to be taken into account, of course. She's an adult. If she really wants you, and you're game—then I'm not going to lean over your shoulder yelling "Foul!" If you're determined to be an adulterer, you'll find a way no matter what anyone says. But, at least, be a practical adulterer. To avoid the usual mistakes, read Chapter 15, "The Married Woman."

When You're with a Date, Don't Come on Strong with Another Girl

This is not only belittling to your date, but it makes *you* look like somewhat of a fool. It casts you as fickle, insensitive, and devoted to status-seeking.

Fortunately, if the gal you're flirting with has any quality at all, she'll ignore you. She'll figure that, even if you're attractive, you aren't worth the time and trouble—you could always do the same thing to her.

Hands off the Other Guy's Gal

Don't mess with the wife or girl friend of a friend or business associate. At best, it's difficult to hide. At worst, it can break up a friendship and leave behind a trail of suspicion, gossip, and hurt feelings.

Your personal devotion to a friend ought to be enough to discourage you from pursuing a woman who is obviously devoted to him. The reasons for laying off a business associate's woman are more subtle. If the man does business with your company and discovers that you are putting it to his wife, he may cut off his orders and give you a bad name throughout the trade.

It can be even worse if the man works within the same organization. I once knew a guy who had an affair with the wife of a fellow worker in his department. It was impossible to hide, and the poor husband was constantly overhearing embarrassing gossip about his wife. He never said anything about it, though. And over the space of ten years he applied himself so diligently to his work that he rose like a skyrocket within the organization. Finally he became president of the company. And he derived immense satisfaction from firing his adulterous friend.

So, if you know what's good for you, you won't "bird-dog."

Don't Say "I Love You" Unless You Mean It

In today's freer society, it isn't usually necessary to lie to a gal in order to screw her. She probably wants it as much as you do. But if she is a bit hesitant, you should resist the impulse to win her over with insincere words of love. Don't obligate yourself unless you really mean it. We all want love, and women are particularly vulnerable to "I love you." But it is not fair of you to lie your way into her bed.

If you can't get her to go to bed and enthusiastically stay there without loading her down with false promises, then you still have a *lot* to learn as a lover.

10.

What Turns a Woman Off

This book has been teaching you how to turn a woman *on*. But what good does that knowledge do you if, without knowing it, something about you turns a woman *off* from the word "go"? You may have a penis like an extension ladder, the charm of the late Ronald Colman, and the endurance to fuck for three days straight—and *still* be a failure with women if you aren't smart enough to avoid punching that female "turn off" button.

What turns a woman off? More than you might think. Women—it should come as no surprise by now—are a completely different sex. The habits and attitudes that make you "Good Ol' Charlie" to the guys at the barber shop are often anathema to women, and you may be missing out on a carload of exciting love-making by failing to perceive and correct those irritations that keep females at arm's length—or beyond.

The intelligent lover realizes that the female is more than two breasts and a vagina—that she's a *person,* loaded down with as many sensitivities as he has. Well, *you're* an intelligent lover, aren't you? You should minimize the possibility of refusal by eliminating as many "turn offs" from your seduction techniques as possible. If you spent as much time figuring out the likes and dislikes of the women you want to lay as you do analyzing the idiosyncrasies of clients, bosses, and fellow employees, you could cut your bedroom losses to nearly zero.

A number of women have confided in me about what men do to upset, antagonize, or distract women from the enjoyment of sex. I've heard some of these complaints so often that I feel I should pass them on to you for study. Being guilty of even *one* of these vices is really going to slow you down sexually.

The Good Samaritan

If you want to *guarantee* striking out with a girl, nothing beats the Good Samaritan routine. The setting is a parked car or the couch in her apartment, and it goes something like this: "What do you mean you won't go to bed with me? I was a big sport, bought you drinks, took you to dinner, paid for movie tickets. I gave you a big evening, baby, and now when I ask you nicely you won't put out a little in return! When I spend my time and money on you, the least you can do is show that you're grateful."

Man, pack it up and take it home! With a line like that you gotta lose. Porfirio Rubirosa and Ali Khan would drop more money on a broad in a single evening than you earn in a month, and *they* were never dumb enough to pull a scene like that. And a good thing, too, or they would have gone back to the Waldorf (or wherever) frustrated. The Good Samaritan routine, however you word it, boils down to this: "Honey, I think you're a whore." Flattery will get you nowhere.

Dating is a social convention. If you are to succeed, you had better play by the rules. The acceptance of your dinner invitation does not obligate any woman to "put out." Sure, you can *hope* and, better than that, you can *try* to seduce her. But does she owe you anything? Certainly—a polite "thanks."

Anyway, be realistic. The fact that you coughed up $3.95 for the salmon croquette special is not going to have any bearing on how irresistible she finds you sexually. When sex is finally included on your American Express card, she'll let you know. Until then, trying to pressure her with the Good Samaritan routine will only make her pressure you out the door.

B.O.

Are you one of those hairy-chested relics from the stone age who think it's effeminate to use a deodorant? Do you believe that a pair of socks isn't really broken in until you've worn it for two weeks without washing? Do you believe that women are like dogs and monkeys, and that only the "smell" of your masculinity will get them in heat?

Well, wake up, friend, and face facts.

There isn't a woman alive who thinks having to inhale rancid sweat at close quarters is exciting. You wouldn't feel like snuggling up to a girl who smelled like the used-uniform hamper of the New York Yankees, would you? Well, she's not going to put her hands and mouth on you if you have a smelly body. At least not voluntarily.

Fortunately, unless you have a peculiar medical problem, eliminating body odor is as easy as baking an instant cake mix. You just add water. If you remember those old Dial soap commercials with the blackboard, you know that a good soap and a stinging shower will wipe all the chalk dust off your body (along with the grime, grit, grease, and odor).

Upon emerging from the shower, dry yourself well under the arms. After waiting about five minutes (for best results), apply deodorant lavishly. The sweat glands are heavily concentrated in the underarm area, so spread the deodorant over the entire armpit and its environs. You are now safe and secure. You have not only banished offensive odor, but you will also be relatively free of those sloppy-looking wet rings under the sleeves of your shirts and that itchy feeling from drops of sweat trickling down your arms and body.

Remember, perspiration odor is tenacious, lingering on when yesterday is but a memory. It clings to underwear, shirts, suits, and coats, and only proper laundering and dry cleaning can completely eradicate the smell once it has dug itself in.

Another form of B.O. that sends a woman scurrying to the opposite end of the couch is *bad breath* ("If she kissed you once, will she kiss you again?"). Certain foods and seasonings, such as garlic and onions, can knock a raccoon on his ass for twelve to twenty-four hours after eating. So, if you have seduction in mind, lay off the smelly foods unless *she* is eating them too.

Another important point. Prince Albert and Four Roses may have an aroma as refreshing as new-mown grass to *you*, but the odor of Scotch and bourbon is unattractive to some women—especially if they are nondrinkers—and cigarettes, pipes, and cigars all leave a very definite odor in clothes and mouth alike. Sound her out on this matter. Leave nothing to chance.

Bad breath can also be caused by decayed

teeth or infected sinuses. Regular trips to the dentist can prevent the first from occurring, and a good physician can help you control the second.

Actually, if you watch TV with any frequency, you are probably free of body odor and bad breath. Commercials have made us positively paranoid about bodily hygiene. Many of us are using four brands of deodorant soap, showering three times a day, combining several brands of spray and roll-on deodorants, brushing with toothpastes that promise to freshen our mouths, gargling with flavored mouthwashes, spraying breath sweeteners between our jaws, chewing mint-flavored gum, popping pills and sucking on mints, and we're *still* insecure. And now they've got our women worrying about whether their vaginas smell!

So don't go crazy over cleanliness or retire from society for fear of offending. Just keep yourself clean. And save the sweat for the playing fields.

The Silent Pressurer

There is a type of guy who just *has* to make it with a girl the first time out. From the minute he meets the girl he thinks, "I won't be able to stand it if I can't get into her pants." And somehow he transmits this attitude to the girl. No matter how gentlemanly his exterior behavior, the girl is aware of his desperation. And she naturally feels belligerent at being put in the position of a villainess for not "giving in" and easing his "suffering."

Like the Good Samaritan routine, this pressure play almost always fails. You just can't try to bribe or bully a woman into the sack and succeed with any regularity. If your natural urges are too much for you at times, do what a number of men do on first dates with desirable (but not yet seduced) females: Masturbate beforehand to relieve some of the sexual pressure so that you can be in command of the evening instead of a beggar.

Scratchiness

Most women have soft, tender skin (*setting number 1* on your Gillette adjustable razor). When you lovingly rub your scratchy, stubbly beard across her sensitive epidermis, she may want to give you a swift kick in the butt. It *hurts,* and it can leave her skin red and inflamed. Just to give you an idea what your stubble can feel like to a woman, imagine the sensation of having your beard rubbed back and forth against the velvety, sensitive skin of your penis. Like a coarse grade of sandpaper, right? So smarten up. Don't turn a girl off with your abrasive kisses. Shave before making love.

Also beware of rough spots on your hands (ragged golf calluses and the like) and jagged fingernails and toenails. And, unless you want to play it like the Marquis de Sade, leave your wrist watch, class ring, cuff links, sharp-edged medals on chains, and eyeglasses on the dresser when you take her to bed.

The Name Dropper

This subject is discussed more fully in the section on Sexual Ethics, but it is worth mentioning here as well. Nothing turns a woman off more than having you name your other conquests. After all, when this romance has died, she doesn't want *her* name to become part of your bedroom patter with another woman. Keep your mouth shut unless you intend to do something constructive with it.

The Grabber

Some men feel that it is imperative to advertise that they are making it with a woman.

Their technique is to clutch and paw their date's breasts, behind, and other extrusions in public, as if to prove that they are terrific lovers. What they *are* proving is that they are crude, insecure, juvenile, and downright *stupid* —because such a display makes a woman feel cheap. And the emotion aroused in the woman is not admiration or desire, but embarrassment and even hate.

It's the old Women's-Liberation bit again. When you paw a woman in public, you are communicating this message: "I think this woman is a *thing;* and she's *my* thing, to use as I please." Show a little respect. You can touch her all you want when you're making love. There's no need to humiliate her in public to demonstrate your manhood.

The Clothes Crusher

Very few men are conscious of the fact that women really *care* about the way they look in public. They go to a lot of trouble to wear the right clothes, the right make-up, the right hairdo. And then some guy comes along at the start of an evening and wraps them up with a kiss and a bear-hug that smears lipstick, musses hair, and turns a neatly pressed dress into a facsimile of a college boy's laundry bag.

Learn to treat your lady's outerwear as if it were another layer of skin (by this, I don't mean you should kiss and lick it—that's fetishism). The smart man recognizes that she probably spent a couple of hours pressing clothes, putting on make-up, and arranging her hair to impress him with her perfect appearance. And he knows she wants to be admired, not mauled.

Save your lust for later.

The Moralist

This is the guy who haunts the fraternity houses at every college in the United States, the king of the "double standard." He knocks himself out pressuring a girl into bed, satisfies himself, and then calls her a "tramp" for being there. This is the fellow responsible for the old feminine war whoop, "You won't respect me if I give in." Girls can get away with this line because there are still plenty of Moralists around —men who actually *won't* respect them if they give in. Strangely enough, the average Moralist makes a big thing about being a supercocksman, and he goes about life as if he is trying to prove to himself that every woman is a whore. Since he tries so hard, he usually succeeds in his strange pursuit.

The Moralist, despite his own masculine breast-pounding, thinks that sex is dirty. And any woman who does it with him is therefore a dirty slut. He wants a virgin for a wife. (Fortunately, he usually gets what he wants: a frigid wife. Fitting punishment.)

A friend of mine who was a member of a fraternity tells me that the Moralist line carries over into fraternity ritual. When a guy is dating a girl on an occasional basis, he is constantly asked (in the grossest manner imaginable) if she is putting out, if he's "getting any." If they pass on to the stage of "lavaliering," it is announced that she has become his full-time whore—which simply means no "bird-dogging" from the brothers, she's all his. But if he "pins" her, the grossness usually subsides, with the house gathering under her window to sing "The Sweetheart of Sigma Chi." And if they get *engaged?* Miracle of miracles, she achieves, retroactively, instant virginity! She becomes the purest of maidens, and any affront to her maidenhood is a matter for the field of honor.

Wacky? Perhaps. But understandable. Most of these men are Moralists, and they *have* to believe that their brother's betrothed is pure and virginal. Even if she *was* a whore last Thursday.

If this bizarre myth of womanhood's purity and the "double standard" were laid to rest when the vows were sworn, it wouldn't be so serious. Unfortunately, most married men are even more firmly attached to the double standard than bachelors! Ask any Elk or Rotarian if it's all right for a man to play around with another woman. And then ask him if his wife is entitled to play around with another man. A good Moralist can talk out of both sides of his mouth, and occasionally out of his ass.

God save us from the hypocrites.

And don't *you* be one.

The Rat

Women are familiar with another type of male we might call The Rat. This fellow employs a technique combining all the pressure methods I've already warned against. How do you smell a Rat? He pulls temper tantrums, sulks, and insults the female to get her into bed. Now and then he succeeds—but what a hollow victory! Who needs sullen sex?

Besides, although she may submit to the Rat's pressure to avoid further unpleasantness, her animosity at being manipulated and used will build up, and sooner or later she'll find some way to use and hurt the guy in return. She may overload his charge accounts, blow the whistle on him to Internal Revenue, bring his son up to be a homosexual (that's *really* putting it to the old man!), or sue him for divorce and win a house and a car and a lifetime supply of money as alimony. What's worse, when she has divorced The Rat, she will probably avoid another marriage (since she has been conditioned by her former husband into believing that *all* men are Rats). So the payments go on for a lifetime. And The Rat will sit in his office and fume at the "frigid bitch" because she, quote, "always did hate men," unquote.

In the long run, then—financially as well as emotionally—learning consideration and good love techniques is the more rewarding course.

The Question Man

This fellow never gets the answer he wants to hear. And he never will, if he persists in asking the question. *Never* ask a girl if you can kiss her, stroke her breasts, go to bed with her, or launch any other delightful experiments.

Deep down she probably has a few leftover notions about being a lady, and asking her outright to do something will make her feel a little cheap. If you put her on the spot, she's almost obligated to say "no," where if you go right ahead, she's quite likely to say "yes." You don't have to ask the question to find out if she's willing—just carry on till you reach an impasse. By this I don't mean rape her (you've eliminated pressure from your technique by now). Simply rely on her response to judge whether she is willing. Actions speak louder than words.

Even the Women's-Lib type, when it gets right down to it, doesn't want to be *asked.* More likely, she'll tell *you* when it's time to make it.

The Bad Timer

Many men get refused not because they are lousy lovers, but because their timing is bad—and this includes thousands of husbands. Tune in to what she's doing a few minutes before you pounce. If the sink is overflowing, your youngest child has just broken and swallowed his front tooth, the oldest is smoking pot on the front porch, and her bridge club is due any moment, and *that's* when you walk in and grab her, is it any wonder that she refuses you? Being rather small-minded and inconsiderate, she may not be able to juggle thirteen crises and ball you at the same time. How would you like it if she walked into your office while you were trying to meet a deadline on an important report and started making passes? Unless you're the coolest exec going, you wouldn't be able to get it up.

Timing is of the essence.

Miscellaneous Turn-Offs

1. *Sloppy table manners.* The guy who sits at a table in a fine restaurant wolfing down his food, washing his hands in his dinner glass, licking his plate, slurping his soup, and reaching across the table like a lumberjack to spear a dinner roll is an embarrassment to his date. Learn the rudiments of table etiquette.
2. *Men who spray saliva when they talk.* Also known as "the spittin' image." No comment necessary.
3. *Men who allow saliva foam to gather in the corners of their mouths.* A relative of the saliva spitter, only without the range. Sounds strange, I know, but one woman I talked to said she ran into this type frequently and that

the habit drove her up the wall. She couldn't keep her eyes off the foam. So be careful, avoid "mad dog" mouth.

4. *Careless smokers, who burn holes in women's clothes, upholstery, and rugs.* These junior pyromaniacs wield cigarettes like torches, dropping ashes on rugs, grinding butts out on table tops, resting lit cigars on the lady's coat. And, to top it all, they give the lady a kiss and an embrace while holding a lit cigarette behind her back. Result: one burned dress. If you smoke, be considerate and be careful. Any rule of Smokey the Bear goes just as strongly in the home as in the forest.
5. *Men who don't say who they are on the telephone.* "Guess who?" Guessing games are strictly for preschoolers. If you're a good lover, she'll recognize your voice eventually, but in the beginning say, "Hi, Mary, this is Bob Soandso."

Of course, if she *still* can't place you, that's another story. Go back to the beginning of the book and start over.

11.

What to Talk About in Bed and When to Laugh

There are three kinds of bed-talk:

1. Pre-sex conversation.
2. The passionate glop that passes for talk *during* intercourse.
3. Post-sex conversation.

Each kind of bed-talk has a different purpose and a distinctive style. You can be a more desirable sex partner just by learning *when* to talk and *what* to talk about in bed. And a happier human being as well, since the things you say in bed can be an important emotional release. In fact, for some men the release of words during intercourse is more important than the release of semen. They may not *know* it, of course. But the Sensuous Man knows it. He knows that getting something off his chest can be just as satisfying as getting off his rocks.

Let's examine the three stages of sexual conversation in the sequence in which they generally occur.

Pre-Sex Conversation

This stage is, in my opinion, the least satisfying for a man. If a man is aroused sexually, he doesn't really feel like talking. He wants to get physical. Most women, however, are not quite as impulsive sexually. They don't generally respond to the abrupt, "Let's ball" approach. They want a slow, natural build-up to sex—a build-up in which words play a critical role. Your words, in conjunction with kisses and caresses, demonstrate your genuine affection. Without the "I love yous" and "You're beautifuls" and "You're warm and tender and excitings," the woman may doubt your sincerity.

Hell, if you're as horny at that stage as I am, *I* doubt your sincerity.

But stop for a moment. You *are* fond of her, aren't you? She *is* attractive, isn't she? Aren't you glad she's there? Then tell her so. Don't lie, of course. Don't turn her off with some elaborate line about how glamorous and sexy she is if she *isn't*. There is a time for the white lie (I'll get to that in a moment), but this isn't it. Just try to express your feelings to her.

This may be a bit awkward, I admit. Maybe you're still in the living room with the lights on, and the heel of your shoe is resting, unknown to you, in the cheese dip on the coffee table, and maybe you were just talking about the fall of prices on Wall Street. But when the time is right, you must give her a signal that the romancing is to begin (if she has not already done so herself). The signal itself may be nonverbal. You might take off your shoes, sigh, and lie back on the couch. Or you might turn off a light or two—any of the methods I discussed earlier in the chapters on sex technique. But this time, concentrate more on the "audio" portion of your approach. Lower your voice to its more seductive and ostensibly sincere level and timbre, take her hand, and begin to make love to her—with words.

What do you say? Well, why not tell her how wonderful the evening has been up to now? Or how much you missed her all day at work. Or how relaxed and content you feel being alone with her. That one is especially successful, for you're saying to her, "You have made an important change in me." It is time to reaffirm the things that attracted you to each other in the first place. Even silliness is in keeping here. Being silly may be the first step in shedding the inhibitions you carry with you all day long—and when you laugh together you have reestablished your intimacy.

That's what it's all about—getting intimate. It is a time for tact. Now is not the time to bring up her faults or reprimand her for her recent failings. And it is not the time to wear your masks and your public personality. *This* is the hardest thing for most men to master. Particularly at this stage, when they are so eager for a successful "seduction," most men rely on some manner of deception in talking with their partners. They think it's so important to be "cool" and "with it" and convincing lest they blow the opportunity. As a result, they feel a little bit phony.

This is a good test of your compatibility with

a sex partner. The more honest and natural you can be with her without jeopardizing your chances of taking her to bed, the better suited you are. If, on the other hand, you have to rely on a line or some phony jazz to get her into bed, then she probably isn't for you (not for long, anyway).

Most men are lousy liars and only mess themselves up when they try to emulate Cary Grant or Marcello Mastroianni.

For example, a friend of mine who thinks he is a sharp operator, reluctantly told me about the night he cornered a beautiful starlet on the couch in her apartment.

"Even if this evening were to end right now," he whispered in her ear, "it would still be the happiest night of my life."

"Do you really mean that?" she said, looking at him with large, luminous eyes.

"May God strike me dead on the spot if I should ever lie to you," he murmured in her other ear.

"Good," she said, handing him his jacket. "Then I won't have to feel guilty about putting you out. Good night."

So my advice to you is to leave the "lines" to the fishermen. Concentrate on the *real* you.

Talk During Sex

It's hard to pinpoint exactly, but at some point in the preliminaries to sex, the conversation begins to suffer. As garments are discarded and flesh is exposed, the long rhapsodic sentences of a few minutes before give way to impassioned and poorly constructed phrases and stray clauses, which yield in turn to barely intelligible grunts and words of one syllable.

It happens, I'm afraid, to the most articulate of us.

Literature has preserved for us the love sonnets of the great poets. But have you ever wondered what they said just before climax? It was probably, "Agggghh! I'm coming! Ohhhh! Fuck!!"

In other words, when it comes to a way with words, sexual intercourse is the great equalizer. Every man a poet.

The reason is partly physical. The more excited you get, the more breathless you become. It's hard to slip in a well-turned phrase between all those gasps, grunts, and moans.

And the reason is partly mental. Fucking occupies so much of your concentration and it exercises so many of your faculties that you generally don't find it practical to settle into the contemplative frame of mind that is favorable to wit and erudition.

The reason is also partly psychological. Those grunts and graphic four-letter words are *exciting.* For most men, "Bird thou never wert" just doesn't make it. "Fuck me, fuck me, fuck me" makes it.

Some women, unfortunately, find such language repulsive, even in bed. They will cringe at "pussy," "cunt," "cock," "suck," and "prick." They may be terrified by the change in your behavior, fearing that they have gone to bed with a vulgar beast.

You could always curb your tongue, of course. But here's my advice: Just explain to your prudish and sensitive woman that you *are,* in a very restricted sense, a *beast* when you make love to her. It's a little like Jekyll and Hyde. By the time you are naked and exposed in sexual embrace with a woman, you have already shed a number of inhibitions. You aren't the trim, dignified Wall Street lawyer any more. You're a hot, sweaty, writhing, pleading, insane *Animal!* And *that's* why you're screaming, "Fuck, suck, prick, cock, cunt, Bang, PUSSY!!!"

Some people will try to tell you that this is the *real* you. I don't know if it is or not (I'm inclined to believe that the *real* you is the rumpled fellow you see every morning brushing his teeth in your bathroom mirror). But it's definitely part of the real you. And once you've convinced your woman that "dirty" language can have its place in bed, and even add to the excitement, you may find her pleading "Fuck me" and moaning "Oh, suck me, baby!" just like they do in those pornographic novels you keep hidden on the shelf in your closet.

Besides, the dictionary term for a "short, sudden emotional utterance" like "Screw me, baby!" is an *ejaculation*.

So what could be more appropriate?

Post-Sex Conversation

At last! That final, *nonverbal* ejaculation. You've come. The sighs and groans of ecstasy have faded away. You lie in bed in your woman's arms. What fulfillment! What contentment! And, if you're like me, you're falling asleep.

WAKE UP! Yawn, blink your eyes, wiggle your toes, but don't drop off to sleep yet. You're right, it *is* the natural thing to do. Sexual release leaves most men satisfied and sleepy. But women seem to live somewhere outside nature, and your partner is going to want more words of love and reassurance from you now that she has given you her all. So, if it was good, tell her so. Tell her how you feel—all that warmth and contentment I mentioned above. Keep touching, fondling, and caressing her; don't roll over and turn away from your partner as if you were finished with her. Your touch now is more precious than ever. This is the time for closeness.

It is also the time for communication. Probably no other occasion is more suited for real communication than the moments following intercourse. Having shared the intimacy of your body, it is time to share the intimacy of your thoughts, your fears, your dreams. And it is time to *listen*, to learn everything you can about the woman in your arms. What are *her* fears? Her joys? What was her childhood like? What was her greatest failure? Success? Ambition?

These little talks can do wonders for your emotional well-being. I speak, as always, from experience. A number of years ago, when the pressures of my career and my inability to cope with minor frustrations seemed about to paralyze me, I started visiting a noted Los Angeles psychiatrist. After only three sessions he told me what was causing me so much grief. It wasn't my problems—they were manageable—but the fact that I kept my problems to myself. "All you really need," he told me, "is somebody to talk to. You have to *share* your feelings with others. I guarantee you'll feel better."

It was a safe bet for the shrinker, since it was obvious I felt better just talking to *him*. And he felt *great*, because he was getting sixty-five bucks an hour for listening.

But I took his advice. I immediately removed myself from his care and took my problems to equally effective and even more satisfying emotional healers: women. For the first time in my life I opened myself up to the women I shared my bed with. And I was amply rewarded. The burden of my cares and fears seemed to dwindle when I shared them with a sympathetic woman. And sharing her thoughts and fears was a welcome distraction from my own problems. And, of course, there was a feeling of closeness and understanding that had been lacking in my earlier relationships with women.

I learned to talk in bed. You can too. You don't have to be glib, just honest and intimate. If you can't drop your masks and voice your real thoughts when you're in bed with your woman, then you're in trouble. You have to learn to give, to trust, and to receive in confidence.

This doesn't mean fishing for compliments or false praise. Women must cringe when they're asked, "How was I?" or "Was I better than George?" I know *I* cringe when a woman asks me, "What do you think of my breasts?" (When faced with such a question, by the way, I *lie*—within the realm of plausibility, of course. I assume most women do the same out of respect for the male's need to feel adequate sexually.)

What should you talk about? You could tell her your latest dream and ask her what she makes of it. Listen to her latest dream and analyze it for her. It doesn't matter if you don't know anything about dreams or psychology—just *talking* will be revealing. Or you might tell a joke, particularly if you are not the type who tells jokes. You can laugh together (especially if you blow the punch line). Tell her about an embarrassing moment in your past. Or simply share whatever crises are plaguing you at work.

Don't feel that you are intruding by telling her your troubles. She needs a shoulder to cry on, too. Just don't be morbid about it. You will find, I wager, that most of your problems are laughable when you share them. Sick humor was invented by lovers talking in bed.

And remember, as long as she's there, you're not alone. That's what women are for.

And that's what men are for.

12.

Her Troubles

Just as women come in all shapes and sizes, they also come with an endless variety of problems, fears, and hang-ups. It is the rare woman who hasn't got *something* eating her, and some women's problems are so weighty as to overshadow everything they do.

Sex, you must remember, is not an isolated part of a woman's life. You have to know more about her than where to put your penis—you must be sensitive enough to recognize and understand what's troubling her and interfering with your mutual sexual happiness.

In this chapter we will look at some of the peculiar problems that plague women, and suggest ways in which the Sensuous Man can help put things right.

Hints on Sacrificing Virgins

"Deflowering a virgin is like fighting a war," a soldier friend of mine once remarked. "It's a dirty job, but somebody's got to do it."

I'm not in agreement with my friend's views on virgins (or war, for that matter), but it's one way of looking at one of woman's most hideous afflictions—virginity. Don't get me wrong—some of my best friends are virgins (small children mostly). But I have to confess to a general prejudice against women who have managed to keep their virtue intact. It seems to me that a woman of any maturity who is by choice a virgin does not make a promising bed partner. If she takes her virginity seriously as a sign of virtue, then she probably has more sexual and emotional hang-ups than I care to bother with. Too many men have been dealt that swift, deadly blow in parked cars in the moonlight: "If I do it with you, you won't respect me."

Gentlemen, you can argue with such a woman. But a lifetime is short. *Forget it.*

There are two other, very practical, reasons that I shun virgins:

1. If she is young enough to be a "legitimate" virgin, then she may be jailbait. I don't intend to sacrifice the Golden Years of my sexuality on the off chance that some nymphet might have second thoughts and blow the whistle on me. I prefer a more mature woman, anyway.
2. Assuming that a woman in her twenties or thirties has spent most of her life marooned on a desert island, or has just issued from a nunnery in protest of institutional chastity, then I will not hold her virginity against her. She simply hasn't had the opportunity. But I still won't choose her as a bed partner, because I might become impatient with her inexperience. Besides, it's a drag doing it the first time.

So much for bad-mouthing virgins. I must remind myself to be more charitable. *Every* woman has a first time.

(To all you virgins out there: If you are sincere in your desire to remedy your unfortunate condition, don't let my defection alarm you. Few men are as jaded as I am, and most will leap at the chance to rupture your hymen—not the recommended method, by the way.)

Whatever your feelings toward virgins in general, some day you may find yourself called upon to deflower one.

1. You may be so young that almost all your prospects are virgins.
2. You may encounter that rare woman whose efforts to divest herself of her virginity have been in vain (a familiar theme in bawdy literature).
3. The woman you have seduced may just turn out to *be* a virgin, to your surprise. They don't wear badges. Unfortunately.
4. You may, for some inexplicable reason, *fall in love* with a virgin. Love is like that.

Here are some suggestions, then, that should make you proficient at deflowering virgins:

First of all, accept the fact that you will have to *modify your technique*, relying more on the psychological and less on the physical. This will not be *your* night to howl. Forget your own sexual desires for once and devote yourself to the successful initiation of your partner. You might even think of the deflowering of the virgin as a religious ceremony or ritual (as it is in many societies).

The setting for the defloration rites should be as private and comfortable and luxurious as possible. This is not the occasion for living dangerously. Don't park in the moonlight, where skills as a contortionist are essential and the friendly neighborhood patrolman may become a spectator. One dolt I know chose as the initiation site his girl friend's bedroom one Sunday afternoon when her parents might be expected to return home momentarily. They did, and he spent a painful period under her bed in the best burlesque-show tradition. After that unfortunate experiment, it's a wonder she didn't remain a virgin the rest of her life!

Be calm, be loving, be gentle. Try to avoid heavy breathing or ramming a stiff penis into her side. You will have to deal with your partner's *fears*—fear of pain (and there may be some pain) and, if she is inexperienced and not knowledgeable sexually, fear of the unknown. Convince her that you will move slowly and carefully, and that you will withdraw if initial intercourse is too painful. Let her *use* you to break the hymen (if it is still intact). This is *her* show, and she must be as confident and comfortable as circumstances will allow.

To expedite matters, you might pour a drink or two down your partner's throat. A small amount of alcohol will desensitize the woman slightly, making whatever pain she may experience less noticeable. Too much alcohol, though, will interfere with what I consider to be the best anesthetic of all—sexual excitement.

Mustering up all your sweet nothings and manual and oral techniques, bring the woman to the peak of sexual arousal. If she is orgasmic, you might consider letting her have one climax to help reduce her tension (although I don't recommend delaying the inevitable too long). The more aroused she is, of course, the more eager she will be to continue and the less noticeable the pain. While manipulating the clitoris, reach down now and then and insert one or two of your fingers in her vagina and gently stretch the opening by pushing the hymen back. If the hymen is not too strong, it may tear under this pressure alone.

When the woman is sufficiently excited, mount her in the face-to-face position with the woman lying on her back, her legs raised and spread as widely as possible to effect easy entry. This position also provides you with excellent leverage. Make sure there is sufficient lubrication (natural or artificial), and very gently insert your penis a short way into the vagina. This is the one time, by the way, that you *have* to have a hard-on. Guide your penis at a slightly upward angle into the vagina. The opening is slightly wider up top.

Warning: In popular male fiction, the hero deflowers virgins by driving his cock home with enough force to rupture dozens of organs, not just the hymen. If you want to *hurt* her, you can ram an andiron up her vagina! Take it easy. Rape is a sorry introduction to sex.

On the other hand, don't be so timid that your partner loses her sexual desire and her confidence in you. You must find some middle ground, judging by her words and reactions. Push slowly and gently (but constantly), continuing to reassure her by word and gesture, until your penis meets solid resistance.

At this point it would be cruel to continue leaning on her hymen, keeping her in pain without actually breaking through. *Now* is the time for that one sharp thrust that novelists are so fond of, that quick surge of pain that is always followed (in books, at least) by a flood of pleasure!

Here's a tip. Just before you make that fateful stroke, *bite her ear.* Or pinch her somewhere, *hard*. She may yelp, but this unexpected pain will distract her so much that she will hardly feel the *real* pain. (I learned this lesson from a doctor who took a splinter out of my leg when I was ten years old. Every time he reached for it with his tweezers, I would back away in fright. Finally, in desperation, the doctor tromped on my foot with the heel of his shoe. While I howled with pain, he deftly pulled out the splinter and I didn't even feel him do it. It's always the pain we *anticipate* that hurts the most.)

Once you have broken through, assess the situation. Lie still for a few seconds to give her a chance to recover from the mild shock and pain of penetration. If she is traumatized and trembling, or hysterical, or unconscious—and none of these is likely—then withdraw your penis and minister to her. But more likely, the real pain over, you will be able to continue to orgasm. But gently. Don't expect her to join you in orgasm (although it is not unheard of, particularly if she has a streak of masochism in her). Save prolonged intercourse for another night, unless her discomfort is truly minimal. (It may take anywhere from two days to a week for her to heal.)

If you are unable to push past the hymen without getting really violent, give up. She should go to a doctor and have it done surgically. It isn't good for a woman to be subjected to a prolonged period of pain in her initial attempts at intercourse. It may color her appreciation of the act later.

If your partner bleeds after intercourse—she may not—have her press her thighs together and lean back on the bed. Then wet a washcloth with warm water and dab her vagina to wipe away any blood or semen. This will also demonstrate that you care for her as a person just as much *afterward* as before. The bleeding should stop shortly. If it doesn't, call the Doc.

Keep in mind that this is a special occasion for your partner. After you have deflowered her, kiss her, fondle her, praise her for her courage, describe the wonderful life of sexual gratification that lies before her, and show her how honored and delighted you are to have been *the first man.* Again, be soft and warm and loving.

And then the ceremony should be capped by some fitting tribute or gesture.

I recommend champagne.

Thawing Out the Frigid Woman

As you may have gathered from the preceding section, I don't take virginity in a woman very seriously. But frigidity is an entirely different matter. The virgin can be "cured" of her condition in a matter of minutes. The frigid woman is not so fortunate. She may spend an entire lifetime without experiencing truly satisfying sexual relations with a man, and a lifetime of frustration is no laughing matter.

To begin with, forget the idea that the frigid woman is emotionally "cold" and unloving. There are such women, but that's not what this section is about. The frigid woman, as defined here, is the woman who *wants* to be a good sexual partner, but is unable to really let go and to achieve orgasm. This country is full of frigid women—one of the "rewards" of our Puritan heritage.

I can't write about frigidity without thinking of one of my earliest love affairs, one that took all my patience and understanding. I met Joy at an outdoor music festival in northern California. She was a tall, slim girl, just turned twenty-one, with beautiful long black hair, a quick smile, and a radiant personality. *She* attached herself to *me* (I can take no credit), apologized for her forwardness, and asked me bluntly and charmingly if I would drive her home. Every bit the gentleman, I agreed.

Instead, we went to my place, where we played records and danced (again at her suggestion). The last dance was embellished with some very long and passionate French kissing while we rubbed our bodies together encouragingly. Reluctantly, in keeping with a promise I had made, I broke up our necking session long enough to take her to dinner. But then it was right back to my apartment, the doors locked, the lights low, soft music from the hi-fi.

Seemingly without inhibition, Joy lay down beside me on the bed, laughing merrily at some witticism, and we began to hug and kiss as before. Real high-temperature stuff. Every time I licked her ear lobe she would shiver with delight, answering my advances with soft caresses and low moans. And then, when I knew the time was ripe (something was ripe, anyway), I cupped a hand over her breast.

She went stiff as a board.

Unless you've made love to a woman like Joy, you have no idea how rigid a woman's body can become. Her limbs were about as flexible as a cold slab of concrete.

She didn't say a word or move my hand

away, but I wasn't so dumb that I couldn't get the message. I rolled over on my back and stared at the ceiling for a few seconds.

"Are you angry?" she asked softly.

I took her hand and gave it a reassuring squeeze. "No, I'm not angry. Just surprised." Which was the truth. Nobody *owes* me sex.

"I just can't," she whispered, choking on the words as the tears began to flow. "I'm sorry, I can't explain it, but I just can't."

Now some men would react to such a confession by sulking or by giving the girl the brush-off. And with another girl, I might have as well. But even as a novice I had a little of the Sensuous Man in me. In other words, I was willing to be understanding—Joy was a person, not a hunk of merchandise. I told her that I wasn't angry; that I found her enormously appealing sexually, but did not intend to force myself upon her; that I thought she was marvelous company for a thousand and one reasons unrelated to sex; that I was sorry if I had offended her; and that I would like to continue seeing her.

It worked. Although there was no sex, the night was saved. We parted amicably with a long, warm kiss and made a date for the next evening.

As the weeks passed, and as Joy and I became more intimate, I learned a great deal about her past. She had been brought up by her mother, her alcoholic father having abandoned them in her infancy. Joy was raised in a strict Protestant environment, and her mother made no secret of the fact that she considered men selfish, cruel, and bestial. Some of this prejudice rubbed off on Joy at a subconscious level. When Joy finally left home, searching for some system of meaningful values, she impulsively joined the Mormon faith. The Mormons were very strict, she told me, on the matter of premarital and extramarital sex. There was no mystery, in other words, to Joy's resistance to sex. Its sinfulness had been drummed into her all her life.

The irony of the situation was this: Joy was not a virgin. Far from it, I was the only guy she *wouldn't* make it with! She told me, quite candidly, that she had slept with a number of fellows, even while she was dating me (although I was the one she loved, she said—and I believed).

Night by night, as we talked it out, I began to understand this seeming paradox. Joy believed so deeply that sex was sinful that she *punished* herself by offering her body up to other men. And, since she loved me, she didn't want to "spoil" our love by having sex with me. "I love you too much to give myself to you," she told me.

I wasn't too thrilled with the way she showed her love, but I was touched nevertheless. I knew that if I insisted she would go to bed with me. But instead I made a little speech: "Joy, I make you the solemn vow that I will never try to force you, by word or deed, to have sex with me, *ever*. And that I will not even *suggest* it or make advances *until*—until you *beg* me. You'll have to *beg* me to make love to you. That's a promise."

How's that for a line? That's why they call me the Sensuous Man.

But again, it worked. I had demonstrated before that my word was good, so Joy was able to relax completely in my company, free of the fear that I was going to try to cajole her into bed. I had proved to her that *I* was moral and considerate and understanding—and, since I was so high on sex, she began to look at it differently, as something positive associated with love instead of something ugly associated with sin.

A month later she smiled wantonly (frigid or not, she was a sexy bitch), kissed me passionately, and whispered in my ear, "Guess what—I'm begging you."

I consider that a high point in my life. But I made it hard on her (and myself). I *really* made her beg. She had to convince me that she really wanted to have sex with me, that she wasn't doing it just because she thought she owed it to me. I gave her every opportunity to back out. But finally, after I had kept her begging and pleading for almost fifteen minutes (this was really a funny scene), I submitted. The Sensuous Man had fallen.

To my delight, Joy turned out to be very uninhibited in bed, whatever her guilt feelings. She was devoted to my pleasure, stroking my penis without urging on my part, and indulging in oral sex. Despite her religious instruction and the shell of repression she had inherited from her mother, Joy was at heart a very passionate girl (my first impression had been correct). We shared a bed for almost a year.

My experience with Joy provides a basic guide for handling the frigid woman. First of all, you must understand that you are dealing with a number of irrational fears, prejudices, and feelings of guilt in the mind of your partner. You must *talk to her,* exposing her fears and guilt feelings for what they are. You can't get anywhere until you get her to recognize that there is something about sex that she finds repugnant or immoral. When that is accomplished, you can start trying to remedy the situation.

Secondly, if your frigid partner is to become orgasmic, you must establish your role as an *unselfish partner*. Many frigid women (like my Joy) are brought up to believe that men "only want one thing from a girl." Until you can get her to trust you, you don't have much of a chance. She'll just think you're trying to get back into her pants.

Thirdly, you must put the focus of attention on *her* pleasure. Emphasize the beauty, the excitement, the satisfaction, the essential goodness of the sexual act. Try to make her understand what she is missing. And devote yourself to her satisfaction. Again, you must convince her of your trustworthiness and your good intentions.

She has to *want* to thaw out, of course. And most of the work she has to undertake on her own. *The Sensuous Woman* is full of exercises, techniques, and advice for the woman who wants to become the sexual equal of any man. It is recommended reading.

Still, all your efforts may not be enough. She

may require professional counseling or psychiatric help. After all, we're asking the frigid woman to

1. Reject her outdated code of morality.
2. Rid herself of her feelings of guilt.
3. Learn to accept her own sexuality.
4. Train her body to respond sexually.
5. Shed her sexual inhibitions.
6. Learn to achieve orgasm through her own efforts.
7. Learn to achieve orgasm with a man.

Brother, it ain't easy. But, with your patience, understanding, and active participation, you can transform the frigid woman into the Sensuous Woman, as I did with Joy. And remember, ridding your woman of every trace of frigidity is as important to you as it is to her. If I had been unable to thaw her out, Joy's inability to achieve orgasm would have ultimately robbed me of most of my pleasure in the act. We would never have been equals between the sheets, and I would have always wondered if, deep down, she still didn't think of men—and me—as something bestial because of their sexual urges. Small matter? Hardly! We men are sensitive too, and we have to believe that our women respect us as much in bed as they do in our nonsexual lives.

In my opinion, to sum up, the greatest single obstacle to sexual fulfillment in modern-day America is the frigid woman—more so, even, than the insensitive and sexually incompetent male.

The true sexual contentment of the American male will come only with the sexual liberation of the American female.

Surviving the Nymphomaniac

Some women (like some men) seem to be missing something inside—a capacity for love, for giving. When a woman attempts to mask this failing through relentless sexual escapades with a faceless parade of men, we call her a nymphomaniac.

The nymphomaniac is out to prove something, mostly to herself. But she fails. Every sexual encounter is a panic-stricken attempt to really "feel something," and each successive failure leads to mounting frustration. The nymphomaniac is not to be envied.

You aren't going to "cure" any nymphomaniac by yourself, no matter how highly you rate yourself as a lover. No penis is big enough or enduring enough to satisfy her. So my advice is to learn to spot the nymphomaniac early and avoid entanglements with her. You have little to gain and much to lose.

How do you identify one? Look for the female counterpart to the Don Juan. She lives by her sexuality, her ability to wear a mask that advertises "hot stuff." But remember the old advertising maxim: "The harder the pitch, the poorer the product." The nymphomaniac's sexiness is skin deep.

Another characteristic of the true nymphomaniac is that she will never "give" you anything; it's all talk. Even in the act of sex, *she* will be draining *you.* It's a fitting reversal of roles, actually. The nymphomaniac is a woman who *uses* men and then discards them. Be wary of the woman who is cold at the same time she is flagrantly alluring, the "sexy bitch" type.

If you get hooked on a nympho, good luck. You will never touch her heart. You will get no love in return. Your sex will be mechanical and cold. And you will never be able to hold on to her. She'll always need another man to boost her ego as a sexually desirable woman.

One word of caution, though. Don't label a woman a nymphomaniac just because she sleeps around. She may just have an excess of affection and an ability to enjoy sex beyond the endurance or desire of most women. She may love life too much to tie herself to just one man, but the small portion of her life that belongs to you may be worth the complete devotion of ten less passionate and less loving women.

But the nymphomaniac? Steer clear.

Over the Hump—or Sex During Pregnancy

Some time or other during your career, you will probably make love to a pregnant woman. It may even be your wife. Well, go to it.

With some slight exceptions, which I shall go into later in this chapter, women are just as sexy during pregnancy as they normally are, and many respond even more passionately than ever before.

The psychological fear of pregnancy is, of course, gone. No precautions or interruptions of any kind are necessary, and she can really let go. She loves being pregnant, her breasts are larger and firmer, and her body is beautifully rounded.

During the first three months of pregnancy, she may be nauseated, vomit often, be bloated and gassy—all effective sex-drive killers. Therefore, if this is true, respect her wishes and refrain from sex at this time should she be disinterested.

Some women (those prone to miscarriages) are forbidden by their doctors to engage in intercourse during the first three months of pregnancy, on the theory that the uterine contractions that occur during orgasm may trigger miscarriages.

Her stage of pregnancy will also, of course, determine her degree of mobility, but normally her passion is as flaming as it always was—often higher because of the increased blood supply to the female organs during pregnancy.

After the third month you can make love in every conceivably comfortable manner. Just be careful not to lean your full weight on her abdomen, or bounce her around as you normally might.

Use your tongue, your hands, your fingers, and your penis as you usually do. Be overly considerate of her feelings and penetrate slowly and only as deeply as she can accept without irritation. Be sure to verbally communicate to her the fact that she is just as desirable as she ever was—and even more so with your child inside her.

If she is more comfortable bringing you to

orgasm orally, forgo the pleasure of coitus until she is in the mood.

As she grows steadily larger, place less and less weight atop her, letting her now lead into positions comfortable to her. Here are some recommended positions for intercourse:

1. Lie on your side facing her back. She is also lying on her side, facing away from you. You can now penetrate the vagina easily from the rear, without placing any weight at all upon the abdomen. This position also leaves your hands free to titillate the clitoris and the breasts (the breasts and the nipples may be very tender and sensitive at this time; therefore, be careful and immediately responsive to any gesture on her part that indicates soreness or discomfort).
2. Have her lie flat on her back at the edge of the bed with her feet supported by a chair or chairs at a comfortable distance to allow you to kneel between her legs. Place pillows beneath your knees to bring your penis to a level with her vagina. You may now penetrate without difficulty (after normal stimulation, of course). This is an excellent position if *either* of you has an unusually large abdomen.
3. The T position is also an enjoyable pregnancy position. Have her lie flat on the bed, her

head as near to the backboard as she can get it. Lie on your side perpendicular to her body. Draw her legs up so that you are between her knees and the bed, with her legs resting on your body. Penetration is now possible and comfortable without pressure.

4. Bend her gently (always gently) over a soft, stuffed chair and enjoy intercourse dog-fashion. It's always great, and you can hold those gorgeous breasts in your hands or play with her clitoris, or both—which I prefer.

All the wonderful sex things you do when she is unpregnant are A-OK, as long as she is comfortable and feeling up to it—mentally and physically.

Vaginismus and Dyspareunia

Vaginismus and dyspareunia are tongue-twisting scientific words that describe fairly rare female problems: involuntary muscular spasm of the outer third of the vagina that prevents or severely limits male penetration (vaginismus) and painful intercourse (dyspareunia).

If you suspect, because of distress during intercourse, that the love of your life is going through the physical and psychological trauma that these diseases produce, *don't* try to cure her yourself. Even the finest seduction techniques will be ineffective. Instead, rush her off to the finest gynecologist in your city.

Dyspareunia, especially, is frequently hard to diagnose, as there are many possible medical malfunctions, such as allergy to contraceptive foams, jellies, suppositories, creams, and the rubber in diaphragms; senile vaginitis; endometriosis; badly performed abortions; broad-ligament laceration syndrome; faulty surgical techniques during hysterectomy; carcinoma of the female reproductive tract; ovarian cysts; uterine tumors—and a hundred other reasons that I don't understand and can't spell. But they all are possible reasons for pain during or after intercourse.

Vaginismus is a lot easier to diagnose and, when treated by a skilled doctor, fairly easily cured.

All this should make you glad you're not a woman, I imagine. But don't feel so smug. Men have their own bouts with dyspareunia. You'll find a brief discussion of the causes and the cures in Chapter 13.

13.

Your Troubles

As if it weren't enough to be intimately involved with all of her troubles, you've got plenty of problems of your own. Not just the "big" concerns, such as getting it up or coming too soon, but a host of special circumstances, both physical and psychological, which call for special handling. They fall into the categories of inconveniences, pitfalls, psychological games, and physiological calamities (and I haven't even included the danger of your turning into a pillar of salt).

None of these problems is insurmountable; some are trivial. Any man with foresight can minimize the hazards of sex and hurdle every psychological obstacle he encounters. He need only be armed with knowledge. And knowledge follows.

Does She or Doesn't She?

Sure she does. It's just a matter of for whom.

You don't hear this question so much any more. But when I was a younger man (not a teen-ager, a young *man*), it was a subject of constant discussion among my fellows. "Does she go down?" one guy would ask. "Like an anchor," another would reply.

The way we looked at it back then, it made no difference *who* was trying to fuck a girl—she was either the type of girl who "did" or the type of girl who "didn't." If she gave in to one guy, it was assumed that she gave in to all. And if nobody in your circle had had her—well, it was simply because she "didn't," and it had nothing to do with the fact that you were a largely repulsive lot.

The same two classes of women exist today, of course:

Class A: Those who *do*
Class B: Those who *don't*

The only difference is that Class A women have come to outnumber Class B women about ten to one. The double standard of morality is breaking down, and fewer and fewer women in the United States are concerned with even *pretending* that they are virgins. Premarital sex is not the scandal it once was; with the coming of the pill it is not the risk it once was; and the term "virgin" has almost become a gross insult to a woman's sexual attractiveness.

As a result, few women today are hesitant when it comes to indulging in sexual experiences outside of marriage. But that doesn't mean they do it with just *anybody*. She may have gone down for your friend Fred, but it was probably because she was very fond of him. Don't expect her to hop into the sack with you at the first opportunity. Most women are very selective about the men they sleep with.

But it *can* be you, of course, as long as you don't take her cooperation too much for granted. Here are a few rules to follow to help insure that the woman who "does" does for you:

1. Be cool and patient. Most women can be tempted into bed subtly, but no law says it has to be the first night. If you fumble and pressure her to go to bed with you an hour after you meet her, she's going to think you're crude (see Chapter 10, "What Turns a Woman Off").
2. Be cautiously aggressive. You don't have to wait for her to take the first step. A woman's whole background, her training, her instincts tell her to wait for your move. As long as you are not too brusque and impatient, she will not be offended by your advances. Her responses to your romancing will clue you as to how fast you can progress.
3. After she finally goes to bed with you, try not to give the impression that you knew she would from the start. Convince her that you are honored and touched that she should single you out for such favors. And, whatever you do, don't say something like, "The guys said you would go down." That's really blowing it.

One final point to remember is this: Even the girl who "does" is telling you something by sleeping with you. She is saying she really finds you attractive. She either loves you, or at least likes you very much. So don't pay her back by telling your friends that she "fucks like a mink."

Show a little gratitude and respect for her gift of love.

Sexual Blackmail

You shouldn't get involved in this kind of distasteful game unless you're married—then, it's too late.

Ever meet the lovely wide-eyed thing who looks as though butter would melt in her mouth? And then she says, "If you take me to Las Vegas, I'll let you!" Pow! Run like hell. If you give in, you lose three ways. She'll never do anything unless you give her something for it —mink, rings, cars, any little thing. She'll always be *letting* you, when she should be wanting you. She'll lose respect for you so fast, you'll think you're already married and bored for twenty years.

At a party, I ran into a group of expensively dressed women in a posh suburban area, whose conversation ran something like this. "John always *bothers* me every Wednesday night." Another remarked, "As long as I get a new car every year, I let him have me twice a month."

I'll bet he doesn't want her twice a month or twice a year—but he's buying her off. Still, he's losing too. She has no respect for him and is crude enough to let the whole world know it. Without respect, love must die. A woman needs . . . cries for . . . a tender, forceful, demanding man. If she can rule or ridicule you . . . you're castrated.

A very good friend of mine used this solution for the "I let him" situation. He arrived home late one night (the kids were in camp), turned on a small light, stripped off his wife's curlers and her flannel nightgown. To her "Have you gone crazy?" he said, "Shut up, you bitch!" He then threw her naked to the floor and fucked the ass off her. Thereupon he told her, "That's the last time I'm ever going to touch your ass, until you beg for it."

She has been a starry-eyed, happy wife ever since, and he's a man again.

Sex should never be treated as barterable goods by either the man or the woman. A woman should never "let" any man make love to her. She should want it, long for it.

She should want you to kiss her and lick her and lay her until she's too tired to move.

The Sensuous Man has too many warm, loving women looking for him to waste his time on a woman with a dollar sign embedded in her cunt.

The Beauty Trap

I've gone out with some of the most beautiful women in the world: celebrities, movie stars, models . . . all types, shapes, sizes, and colors. While many of them are warm, giving, and wonderfully exciting in bed, too often they depend entirely on their looks and never involve themselves in the art of good love-making. Slim-hipped, flat-chested models particularly operate on the mistaken assumption that men will overlook all their shortcomings in exchange for the "prestige" acquired by squiring them around town.

Too many of them give nothing. Their make-up can't be smudged. Their hair can't be mussed. Their skin can't be the least bit irritated. Their timetables and their careers come ahead of everything else.

Don't you play a poor second to anyone!

There are some beautiful, intelligent women around who will welcome the Sensuous Man into their lives and their arms, who will share deep emotions and passions without picking the times and places for their appearances and disappearances, but they are rare.

I remember one beautiful little starlet-model in Hollywood who was my prearranged blind date when I unexpectedly flew in from London. We went to a great party at the home of a world-famed writer. My date was attentive as hell while I introduced her to celebrity after celebrity but, between hanging on my arm and dashing after every career possibility, she revealed her true self—which wasn't really very pretty. She didn't overlook a single director or producer who might give her a "leg up," so to speak.

Oh, yes, she was perfectly willing—perhaps even anxious—to go to bed with me when we arrived at her apartment. I politely declined, to her utter astonishment—knowing full well that the "What will you do for me?" entry price of admission would bar the possibility of free and joyous sex.

Some men require a gorgeous possession to hang on their arm—to impress the gang, to bolster the ego.

You're paying an exorbitant price for a beautiful face or a fabulous body, if underneath she is merely a shallow, clinging, social-climbing bitch whose only concern may be to find out how soon you will take her to the latest "in" restaurant or club where she can be seen.

A good friend of mine—handsome, wealthy, a supposed swinger—invariably falls for this type of girl. Why he needs the "ornament" I'll never know. One evening recently, his latest gal was so peeved because he didn't take her to the opening of a new private discotheque that she threw a tantrum at 3:00 A.M. when they were both pretty high, and sent him home. Somewhere in the Canyon he went off the road and was almost killed.

He still hasn't learned though. My theory is that my friend is *afraid of failing* in a relationship where he would be expected to give and receive love freely, so he opts for a showy substitute that gives him ego satisfaction instead. It is sad indeed that he is cheating himself of much of the pleasure of living.

The peculiar selfishness of a certain type of beautiful woman produces some really bizarre behavior at times. Let me tell you the incredible story of a woman so beautiful and so easily recognized that mere mention of her name can make a man's head spin. This exquisite femme fatale of the film world is so narcissistic that she dictates the manner in which she permits men to make love to her. Her agent is dispatched to the man she is eyeing and he is advised that he may go down on her any way he can imagine —she especially likes chocolate syrup and warm champagne—but no fucking . . . and, of course, no satisfaction for him. She comes. He doesn't. Lovely bitch, eh what?

While the Sensuous Man can excite most women, the beauty traps simply aren't worth the effort. Many starlets and models are just plain lousy in the hay.

Never forget that love and loving can make a plain woman beautiful so, if that's your bag, you can create your own beauty trap—filled with good sex and generous loving.

Tears—and How to Deal with Them

Most men are at a loss when a woman begins to cry. Tears are a frequent female emotional outlet (and occasionally her most lethal weapon). The average guy, at the first sign of tears, goes on the defensive: He stands there wringing his hands, wondering what it is he's done, or what it is he is *supposed* to do. He finds it difficult to comprehend why a perfectly lovely, normal, sensible, and apparently reasonable woman should burst into a sudden fit of weeping.

The first thing that comes to mind is that she is crying because of *you*—something you did, said, or forgot. But such may not be the case at all. She may be crying because her zipper is stuck, her stocking has a run in it and you're late to the theater, her hairdo keeps collapsing, or her period is due any minute. Or she may actually be *happy* and showing it through tears. Strong emotion of any kind makes some women cry—particularly at weddings.

Then again, she may, indeed, be sad. If you are leaving on a trip, the prospect of separation may bring a tear or two at parting. She may cry because of some failure of her own that she imagines is making her less than a perfect partner for you. Or she may simply be depressed, as we all are from time to time.

If you diagnose her tears as the symptoms of one of these circumstances, go to her and comfort her. Make her feel wanted and loved. Kiss her tears away gently and hold her close. Tell her that nothing is important but her happiness. And patiently weather the deluge.

If, on the other hand, *you* seem to be the source of her unhappiness, try to find out what you've done to upset her. And if you have really fouled up—and know it—apologize, promise to reform, and ask her forgiveness (or at least her understanding, if you are reluctant to grovel).

But try to find out *what* it is she's crying

about. Otherwise she'll discover that she can make you feel miserable any time she turns on the tears.

And that's the real danger. Because some women—very few, thank God!—use tears as a weapon. They'll use tears to badger you, pressure you, make you feel like a heel, or distract from their own failings. They'll cry when they want something. They'll cry when they don't want something. They'll cry every time you do *anything* not precisely in keeping with their wishes.

How should you handle the Wily Weeper? One way is to laugh right in her tear-streaked face. Yes, I said *laugh.* Nothing will make this type of woman stop crying more quickly. She simply won't be able to believe that you are capable of laughing at her in that state, and the shock will block the flow of tears. She may become furious and throw a potted plant or a lamp at you, of course—but she'll stop crying.

Another technique would be to cry along with her. I can't really predict the ultimate consequences of this tactic, but at least your behavior would be curious enough to halt *her* crying. Any response other than your terrorized acquiescence will have some effect on the Weeper, who is only crying because she knows it *works.*

Still another shock technique for handling the hysterical crier is to throw water in her face. The short-term result may be blind fury on her part, but you've got to break her of her habit of manipulating you with her tears.

Before you employ any of these techniques, *be sure* that she is really using her tears to force your hand in some way. If her crying is sincere and she is really upset, laughing at her or dousing her with a bucket of water will give her the impression that you are a callous brute. And that won't help your relationship any.

But remember: If you consistently "give in" to tears, you'd best purchase a serviceable raincoat. Because every time you say no—you'll get wet.

Every Twenty-Eight Days! Red, Red Everywhere

Men shave and women have menstrual periods, and *vive la différence* . . . but sex can go on regardless.

There are many ancient taboos against making love while a woman is menstruating. They're all nothing but superstitions or old wives' tales. A woman is usually tremendously sexy just before, during, or immediately after her period.

The choice of having intercourse or not having intercourse is almost entirely up to the man. As it is a natural part of her bodily function, the woman will rarely object and, if he has no hang-ups, it can be a really exciting episode in an affair.

I don't particularly recommend intercourse during the menstrual period if it is the first time for you to make love with the lady but, once you are on intimate terms, why simply protect the bed sheets, damn the tampons, and plow right ahead.

While she may be very flattered that you want her in this condition, she knows she is not at her most desirable, so be gentle and diplomatic. (Some gals have really rough days during their periods, so don't push it if she is reluctant.)

Titillate her clitoris (I don't suggest your tongue at this time) with your fingers, as you normally would, stroke her breasts, treating the nipples very tenderly as this is another of those times when they are extremely sensitive. In other words, do everything you both like to do. Your only restriction is that you should avoid moving from one location to another, as you don't want to stain anything.

Wait until the last moment, when you are both pretty hot and bothered, before you ask her to remove the tampon. (If you're in the mood, pull the string yourself, but drop the tampon carefully on a prepared pile of tissues.) Because the tampon has a drying effect, moisten your fingers with saliva, vaseline, K-Y jelly, or nonallergenic cream, and massage her clitoris for a moment or two until she's wet and wanting. Kiss her breasts and tell her how exciting she is and show her that you love to love her no matter what. She'll adore you, and her response may be a great deal more passionate than you anticipated.

A woman is, after all, a beautifully feminine thing, and her period is just a small part of that femininity.

She Wants to Get Married— and Your Wife Won't Let You

A familiar character in the movies is the silver-haired businessman whose slinky, sultry mistress keeps asking, "Have you told her yet? Are you getting your divorce?"

The freewheeling patriarch usually replies,

"Uh . . . er . . . well. . . ." A quarrel ensues. And a situation develops where the adulterous husband must decide either to (1) drop his mistress, (2) divorce his wife, (3) murder his mistress-turned-blackmailer, or (4) murder his wife.

Naturally, the businessman is distressed at this turn of events. Things were going so *well* for him—the respectability of the wife and kids at home, the excitement of the mistress in their love nest. Why, he agonizes, did it have to change?

The reason is usually this: The philandering husband, fearing that the mistress may turn off the sex, allows her to get the impression that he is going to divorce his wife of twenty years, abandon his children, and run away to marry *her*. This keeps the mistress satisfied and generous for a while, but soon he has to start making out-and-out promises which he inevitably breaks. And finally he resorts either to (1) giving up his sex life, (2) sacrificing his respectability, or (3) and (4) earning himself a forty-year stretch in the state penitentiary.

You, if you are married, may find yourself facing a similar decision—unless you take the proper action at the *beginning* of your adulterous affair. The rule is simple: Don't make promises you can't keep. If you follow this rule, you won't get into deep trouble.

This advice is easier said than taken, of course. Little girls want pretty things and pretty smells and to be cuddled and kissed—but most of all they want to be wives. *Your* wants are more basic, so you may weaken and let a promise slip off your tongue while you're panting heavily with desire. And then you're dead. And you deserve it.

You can't really blame her. Here you are, one of the world's most sensuous men, holding her in your arms, telling her beautiful things, kissing her, fondling her, driving her out of her mind! After that kind of treatment, do you expect her to "understand" that you have to go home to your nagging old wife? Forget it. She wants you, *you!* So if you want to keep her (and keep her happy), you're going to have to be a combination of Casanova, Paul Newman, and Winston Churchill.

The rule here, as it is so often in sexual matters, is *honesty.* Play it straight with a gal and she'll respect you for it. But lie and she'll end up hating you. Make it plain from the start that you are *not* going to divorce your wife.

You don't have to go *crazy* with honesty, though. You might tell her (a tear sliding slowly down your left cheek) that your wife is incurably insane and you *can't* divorce her. That's a lie, but a different kind of lie. Know the difference: Lie about your home situation, but don't lie to her with false promises.

Don't tremble or whine or placate her with excuses and small deceits. Be bold. If you're faced with a "your wife or me" situation and you know darned well you're not going to leave Maggie and the four kids, strike back with, "I love you, I'll always love you, but I can't leave the children—" [Not the wife, the *children.*] "—The sun and the stars will go out of my life without you and I may not survive, but if that's what you want—go now and be happy."

Chances are she is bluffing anyway. But, in any event, this performance (if you can deliver it without cracking up) will break her heart. She may wind up apologizing to you for being so mean and selfish.

Naturally, you will forgive her. Immediately fling her onto the nearest soft horizontal surface and show her how deeply grateful you are—deeply, deeply, deeply.

Crabs, Trench Mouth, and Venereal Disease

Very few endeavors in life are without hazard. Skiers must be wary of avalanches; waterpolo enthusiasts risk drowning; skydivers are potential pancake-people; smokers brave cancer; office seekers risk defeat; and we who insist on inhaling city air are sacrificing, perhaps, years of our lives.

Sex is no exception to this unpleasant tendency. But happily the physical risks involved in intercourse are relatively minor when compared with more adventurous pursuits, such as motorcycle racing, skin diving, bank robbing, or drinking river water. Minor, at least, if you are well informed and sensible enough to seek medical help when your sexual adventures produce something you didn't bargain for.

Crabs, for instance. These are lice which specialize in the pubic area and, although I have never had them, I gather that they particularly favor people who labor under unhygienic conditions. But they can latch on to *anyone*—they have no respect for "classy" folks or intellectuals.

So, if you want to play host to itchy, biting parasites, push fearlessly ahead wherever opportunity beckons. If not, you can probably shun the little devils by avoiding visits to waterfront dives and slum brothels. But, even if you know that your sex partner is untainted, remember that you can both get crabs from the locale in which you make love (for instance, an unsanitary bed in a transients' hotel, an unchlorinated swimming pool, or a bathtub that contains traces of a previous bather's pubic hair).

If you do find yourself host to a few hundred lice some not so fine day, take a quick trip to your friendly neighborhood druggist and confess all. He won't be too abashed to sell you a good-sized bottle of smelly ointment that, when applied, will have your crabs dropping like flies. Read the instructions carefully, by the way, or a couple of weeks later you'll have a new set of friends feeding off you.

Another minor affliction of which to be wary in your sexual encounters is Vincent's angina. Actually, Vincent's angina sounds pretty sexy. But the romance in that name is more than compensated for by the more common term for the condition—trench mouth. Trench mouth is a contagious disease caused by a bacterium and marked by ulcerations of the mucous membrane in the mouth. It can be treated effectively with antibiotics, but I think it's wiser to avoid the disease altogether, don't you? My most transparent solution is to avoid intimate contact with seedy-looking women. But trench mouth is not always that advanced, serious, or obvious. And anyone can get it. So about the best you can do is make sure that your women practice good oral hygiene and that you do the same. And if you *do* get trench mouth, get rid of it before you kiss again (unless it's an ex-wife who is putting the screws to you, and even then . . .).

But these are piddling concerns. The real hazard of sex is venereal disease. Public health officials don't look upon VD as a disease which individuals pick up; they think of it as a *social* affliction and use the word "epidemic" to describe its spread in recent years. Unfortunately, the public campaign waged against syphilis and gonorrhea (and the less-well-known lymphogranuloma venereum, chancroid, granuloma inguinale, and vaginitis) seems morally motivated, concentrating more on stamping out *sex* than fighting the diseases themselves.

So, instead of disseminating information about how to avoid venereal disease, or where to go for help, overzealous officials prefer to print up "scare literature" for the schools and the ghettos, suggesting to the young, the poor, and the ignorant that premarital or extramarital sex almost inevitably leads to mental illness, blindness, destruction of the central nervous system, and epilepsy. This doesn't do much to stop the spread of venereal disease (since it makes victims ashamed to report the symptoms), but it sure scares the hell out of a lot of parents.

Actually, syphilis and gonorrhea are easily treated if caught in time, and the symptoms are readily apparent. If a lesion (a moist, painless chancre) appears on your genitals, if you have painful erections, if you experience a burning while urinating, or if your urine turns a thick, greenish yellow—then go right to your doctor. He'll take care of it. Even if there is doubt in your mind, *see your doctor*. Many of the primary symptoms of syphilis disappear, only to be replaced later by more serious complications.

How do you avoid venereal disease? The easiest way is by avoiding sex. This, obviously, is a totally unacceptable answer.

A more realistic approach is to use a condom if you are having intercourse with a woman whose condition you have reason to question. And be sure to wash your genitals thoroughly with soap and water after intercourse.

It isn't that easy, of course, to size up a girl as a prospective carrier of syphilis or gonorrhea. Dr. Albert Ellis suggests in *Sex and the Single Man* (page 145) that venereal diseases are rare

> . . . among nonpromiscuous persons from middle-class, college-level, professional-type backgrounds.
>
> On the other hand, they are much more common among promiscuous persons from lower-class backgrounds and among severely disturbed individuals. If, therefore, you usually restrict your sex activities to fairly well-educated girls who you know, in their turn, limit their sex participation to relatively few partners, you will have little chance of contracting any venereal disease.

Well, maybe. Frankly, my experience is that the clap respects no man's bankroll or position in society. If you fuck around, you can get VD, no matter how pure and unsullied you think she must be because she graduated from Smith or Vassar.

But get one thing straight—it *is* a woman who will give you VD, not a plumbing fixture. That same very wise old medical captain, mentioned in my chapter on Masturbation, also gave us this word of advice: "When, at any time, you men notice rashes or canker sores in the pubic area or on the penis, report to the medics immediately to let them check it out—the sooner the better. And, if any of you guys tell me that you got VD from a toilet seat, all I can say is: That's a hell of a place to take a woman!"

In short, the more you sleep around, the better your chances of acquiring a venereal disease. And the more *she* sleeps around, ditto. Which, on reflection, is one good thing about a virgin. She won't have a venereal disease unless *you* give it to her. (By the way—*don't.* If you have VD, it is your moral responsibility to abstain sexually until it has cleared up *completely.*)

But, if you observe good habits of hygiene and are selective about your sex partners, you have little to fear. The chances of catching a venereal disease are slight. And, even if you *are* the unlucky guy who becomes a statistic, the cure is relatively routine. I, for one, worry more about flying in the new 747's than I do about VD.

Forewarned and prepared, the Sensuous Man fucks fearlessly.

Male Dyspareunia

Both men and women, as noted earlier, can experience painful intercourse. The all-inclusive term to describe this unfortunate condition in men is *male dyspareunia.*

The most common of these varied ailments,

and the least serious, is the testicular vasocongestion familiar to many young men as "aching balls." It is caused by maintaining a high level of sexual excitement for a fairly long period of time without relief—for instance, by reading pornographic literature in the attic without jacking off (horrors!), or petting for hours without the relief of orgasm. The cure is uncomplicated and instantaneous—ejaculation by any means. As a man ages, this symptom of sexual frustration generally disappears, or at least lessens in severity. (This is one form of dyspareunia where intercourse is not the cause of, but the cure for, a painful condition.)

Here are some other varieties of dyspareunia which can cause men pain before, during, or after intercourse:

1. Phimosis—a foreskin that cannot be contracted over the glans penis. The cure is circumcision.
2. Hypersensitive glans penis—some men have penises which are irritated by contact with almost anything, including their own clothing. Containment in the vagina can be very painful. There are preparations for such men to "desensitize" the glans area.
3. Penile "trauma"—an erect penis can be traumatized if it is struck sharply, or if the female

sits directly on it with all her weight. The result may be a permanent downward bowing and considerable pain during intercourse or masturbation.

4. Post-gonorrheal burning—men who have had gonorrhea may experience a sharp burning sensation when urinating or ejaculating.
5. Irritative reactions to vaginal infections—some men experience a blistering of the glans due to infectious bacteria in the vaginal environment.
6. Irritative reactions to chemical agents—both men and women can experience discomfort due to chemicals in contraceptive jellies, foams, and creams. And some men react painfully to female douche preparations.

There are many other causes of male dyspareunia. The only thing you really need to know is: If you hurt, go to the doctor. Don't be a martyr. And, remember, pain is not the natural order of things in your sex life. If it hurts, something is *wrong*.

14.

The Women's Liberation Movement —and You

I have a recurring nightmare in which the woman to whom I am making passionate love suddenly cries out, "Male chauvinist pig!" and kicks me out of bed.

It could be worse, of course. The more militant members of the contemporary Women's Liberation movement would settle for nothing short of castration with can openers, scissors, and rusty razor blades.

But let's forget about the ultraradical feminists, the dykes, and the crazies. Let's confront the issues:

Women claim that most men perpetuate a "double standard" of sexual morality. *They are right.*

Women claim that most men view women solely as sexual objects to be "used." *They are right.*

Women claim that most men are totally selfish in bed, exploiting their partners to reach orgasm and then ignoring the woman's need for sexual satisfaction. *They are right.*

At heart, that's what this book is about. That's what *The Sensuous Woman* was about—the concept that in sex (and, it is hoped, in all other aspects of life) the woman is a *completely equal partner.* She should benefit from sex just as much as the male.

In an earlier chapter, you will remember, I said that "the greatest single obstacle to sexual fulfillment in modern-day America is the frigid woman." I don't blame women for that. We men deserve *more* than our share of the blame.

It's time for soul-searching. Look at yourself. Maybe you *are* a male chauvinist pig!

Do you hide behind the newspaper all day long, answering her questions with grunts and shoulder-shrugging, and then demand sexual satisfaction at bedtime?

Do you fly into a rage when, on rare occasions, she just isn't in the mood for sex?

Do you put your penis in your woman's vagina after only a few moments of foreplay (hardly long enough to arouse her sexually)?

Do you ejaculate after only a few seconds and then make no effort to satisfy the lady, leaving her physically and emotionally frustrated?

Do you complete intercourse and then immediately roll over and go to sleep with hardly a tender word or caress for her?

Do you rebuke her for her "coldness" when she is unable to have orgasm because of your "slam-bang" technique?

If you can answer "yes" to one or more of these questions, then you *are* a little bit of a pig—male chauvinist or otherwise. I would guess that unfortunately the *majority* of American men fit into this category, especially those men who consider themselves particularly "masculine."

This selfish, male-oriented attitude has rubbed off on many American wives (particularly, we are told, in the lower economic and educational strata), who approach sex as a distasteful ordeal they must regularly endure in order to "serve" their husbands. Is it an exaggeration to label such an arrangement as a form of "slavery"? I think not.

To be a Sensuous Man, you must respect your woman. You must consider her sexual pleasure as important as (or more so than) your own. You must treat her as a whole person, and not as a sophisticated masturbation machine.

Times are changing. Today a great number of attractive and rational women are committed to Women's Liberation and dedicated to righting the imbalance between the sexes. Any man who is either unaware of or unsympathetic to these sentiments will be at a disadvantage if he attempts to romance a woman who is sensitive to what she considers symptoms of male supremacy.

For example:

—She will resent being treated as a child, both in public and in private.

—She may resent being called a "girl" when she is forty-eight years old.

—She may resent your introducing her as "Jane" to men who are always "*Mr.* Smith" or "*Mr.* Wallace."

—She will be agitated if you constantly make generalizations about women that stress their inferiority.

—She will resent your mocking her efforts to be creative (painting, writing, and similar endeavors) instead of adhering strictly to the housewife-and-mother stereotype.
—She will resent your belittling her political convictions as if she were somehow less qualified to make judgments than you.

In short, she will be sensitive—perhaps unreasonably sensitive. If such is the case, you don't have to be a spineless "yes man" to her paranoia. *Tell* her that you think she is being overly sensitive. But be direct and serious about it. Don't "humor" her and smirk behind her back.

If you are infatuated with a Women's-Lib female and want to gain and hold her respect and love, it wouldn't kill you to join the movement yourself if you're politically oriented. The very least you can do is vote a deserving woman into office, write letters urging your representatives to pass laws granting women equal protection and opportunities (and shrewdly send a carbon to *her*), support companies that pledge themselves to fair employment practices, and *listen* when she talks about her problems as a woman.

You should be thinking along these lines even if the woman you love is *not* the Women's-Lib type at present. Most women are still very tradition-bound (as are most men) and will express contentment with their present lot. But even the most devoted and submissive female may be nursing a grudge or two and, after reading about the "revolution," hearing about it from friends, and watching it on TV, she may finally muster up the courage to take a stand. The first place she's likely to make that stand is in the bedroom, demanding an equal role in your sex life. And if you aren't ready for that, you're in trouble.

But you shouldn't have to wait for *her* to take that first step. You should liberate her yourself. And, believe me, it's no sacrifice at all. The lover of the sexually liberated woman benefits in a number of ways, most importantly:

1. Since she is a partner, he doesn't have to do all the work.
2. He doesn't have to accept 100 percent of the responsibility for the success of each lovemaking session.
3. He will have a freewheeling, impulsive, highly charged partner unafraid of doing anything that will excite him.

If you follow the rest of the advice in this book, you will definitely not be a male supremacist (except to those females who believe that *any* sex is exploitative). And this is all to the good. It shouldn't be too hard for you to figure out that, if you are truly the Sensuous Man, you have nothing to lose from the liberation of the American female—and a world to gain.

15.

The Married Woman

For the last ten years I've made it a rule never to go after married women. There are enough sexy women around who are unencumbered by jealous and possibly even homicidal husbands to last me a lifetime.

Adultery may not be for you either, but we both know that at one time or another it seems to have an irresistible appeal to one or both partners of most marriages. I'm not one to argue with statistics. Let's face it, marriage today is becoming more and more a simple legal contract, routinely terminated by mutual consent of both parties (although this is still messy in many states). The ease with which marriages can be terminated—as the majority are eventually—is just a reflection of the fact that people often change in their feelings toward one another. Love sometimes fades within marriage, love sometimes blooms outside marriage.

Besides, more and more married couples are taking "infidelity" as a matter of course, a way of bringing sexual variety into their marriage. Romantic? Maybe not. But there's no denying the trend.

Another consideration is *adventure*. Many men like to live dangerously, and only the fear of discovery really turns them on. So making it with a married woman, for such men, is just an extension of having a quickie at a party with the bedroom door unlocked, or getting a blow job in the vestibule of a moving train—there is always the fear of discovery and the sense of wickedness. Many men go wild at the thought of sleeping with married women who wouldn't excite them at all if they were still single. It's part of the "grass is always greener" syndrome. The supposedly unavailable is always more desirable than the easily attainable.

Finally, of course, there's that word "adultery," which I think is one of the most irresistible words in the English language. It has such a sensationally evil and titillating sound to it! I suspect that the name we have given this forbidden sexual activity is in part responsible for its popularity.

So, if you want to make it with a married woman, great! That's between you and the lady.

Here's some advice, though. If the married woman has turned to you, it's probably because she's looking for something her husband can no longer give her—excitement, romance, adventure. You must treat her like a woman (or a mistress)—anything but a wife. Don't take her for granted—that's why her husband is at home with the TV dinner.

In bed, be adventurous—daring. Try all those positions that her husband considers too far out. After all, if she wanted the Missionary Position every night, she would have married a missionary. Hell, if she wants to feel wicked, let her *be* wicked! Anything goes. That's what adultery is for.

Where to make love can be a problem with the married woman, particularly if it is inconvenient for you to be seen together. If you are a bachelor with your own place, fine. No sweat. Otherwise, you might have to go for a drive in the country or rent a room in a hotel or motel. Find out how she feels about the subject. Some women find a motel room a sexy environment, but others feel cheap in one. Don't turn her off by making the affair tawdry.

If she *does* find the hotel or motel acceptable, and you want to check in and out without drawing attention or risking discovery, follow these bits of advice:

1. Always pay cash. It may be difficult to break the expense account habit, but credit card receipts are a permanent record of your adulterous activities. If you are married, your wife may puzzle over that "hotel room for two" that American Express calls to her attention. And a few eyebrows may be raised at work if you try to push such an item through expense-account channels.
2. Don't arrive at a motel in separate cars. Few couples travel together in such fashion.
3. Try to scrounge up a little more luggage than a fifth of Scotch and two ham and cheese sandwiches in a brown paper bag.

4. If you have monogramed luggage, remember to sign the register with a name that matches.
5. Suggest that she dress conservatively. When you're trying to slip through a hotel lobby unnoticed, it doesn't help if she's wearing her zebra-skin poncho, sequined body stocking, and gold lamé boots.
6. If room service is delivering something, have her slip into the bathroom until the bellhop has left. But tell her *why* she has been banished to the bathroom. It doesn't do any good if she starts running water or singing in the shower.
7. If the telephone rings, *you* answer it—even if she's your secretary in real life.

Another love-nest possibility is the apartment of a friend who lends you his keys and promises not to show up some afternoon or evening. But this solution has its hazards as well. The friend might realize that he has forgotten his all-weather coat and just pop in for a second —while you and your married woman are cavorting naked on his coffee table.

More importantly, using a friend's apartment may strain your relationship with the friend, particularly if you make a practice of leaving travel folders on his desk or signing him up for the Monday Night Bowling League. He's going to suspect that you value his apartment more than his friendship, and he may resent being made to feel guilty because he wants to spend a night or two at home. After all, it's *his* apartment.

So be circumspect in asking such favors. The best time is when your friend is going on a legitimate vacation and definitely won't be inconvenienced by your sordid carryings-on. (Remember also that bringing a friend into your illicit affair makes it that much less of a secret. Be sure you can trust him to keep his mouth shut.)

Keep in mind when arranging the rendezvous that oversecrecy can call attention to itself. You may have worked out some elaborate plan for meeting your beloved at a mountain resort, but what good is it if it demands three days of travel by divergent routes, involves the logistical support of the Seventh Army, and makes all the morning papers? Besides, the best-laid plans for secrecy are often in vain—that quiet little monastery in Quebec you chose for a love nest may just turn out to be the place her husband has chosen for a weekend retreat.

Don't fuck her in her own home unless she says it really turns her on. Most women will be uncomfortable at home for fear that the kids will come home too early, a neighbor will pop in, the milkman will see you and get jealous—and there's always the chance that she'll forget to empty the ashtrays, leaving your smelly cigar smoking in the living room for her husband to discover when he comes home. And, oh yeah—remember her husband? You don't want to play that old closet routine, do you?

Besides, it's in bad taste to make love in her home, and she may feel guilty about it. Her home is something she shares with *him,* and she may come to consider you an intruder in what was once a happy marriage (she may even *blame* you for the breakup!). But, like I said, she might get turned on by that instead—making it in *his* bed. Watch out, though, if she asks you to wear his pajamas.

When calling her at home, don't hang up if her husband answers. That will only make him suspicious. Instead, pretend you're drunk and trying to phone your mother in Green Bay, Wisconsin. It's not advisable, of course, to call her at home at *all* if you can avoid it. At the very least, arrange for times when it is safe to call.

Follow the same order of thinking at the office. Unless you have a line that is truly private, discourage her from calling you there often. And don't ever have her meet you at work.

Office gossip can spread to the far corners of the earth with the speed of a microwave relay system.

If *you* are married, here's a reminder that can be crucial: Be sure to readjust the seat belt in your car to where your wife had it. I know a guy who was ultracautious about spotting telltale female hairs on his overcoat, wiping make-up off his collar, and washing off all traces of lipstick—but he was tripped up when his chubby little wife couldn't latch her seat belt. She immediately knew that someone "slim" had shared that seat with her husband. And he was caught without a convincing alibi.

Another very important point to remember in your affair with the married woman is that you may have to be more demonstrative of your love than usual because most of your meetings will be for the sole purpose of having sex together. She will need constant reassurance that you value her as a person, not just as a convenient "quickie." Take her disposable presents like candy or a good cheese; talk to her more than you would a casual girl friend; and every now and then, for variety, meet her secretly for some purpose *other* than sex. It will give the relationship some balance, demonstrate that you find her a thoroughly attractive companion, and make your next sexual rendezvous all the more satisfying.

Finally, unless you plan to marry her, don't get involved in her marital problems. Make it clear that your affair is something quite distinct from her marriage. If she wants a warm sexual relationship with you, fine. But if she wants a shoulder to cry on, make sure that that's *all* it is. Don't try to mix the roles of adulterous lover and family friend. That can only end in bitterness and bruised feelings.

If you manage it right, the affair with the married woman can be almost ideal. After all, such a lady is usually mature and experienced sexually. And, since her home life is completely separate, it is the "good things" that she will experience with you, while her husband has to worry about the fact that she snores, is three months behind on the laundry, and doesn't seem too interested in sex.

Your only worry is discovery. But then, fear of being found out, remember, is what makes your affair an adventure.

16.

The Chandelier vs. the Bed

It is said that there's a time and a place for everything, sex included. But that doesn't mean the time must *always* be 10:30 P.M. and the place *always* your bedroom. There's nothing wrong with adding fun and adventure to your sex life by stepping out now and then to make love in some strange exotic location. The only compelling reason for screwing in some secret place is that it is just plain *fun*. But it is also worth noting that sexual variety can keep a relationship from growing stale or slipping into dull routine.

What do I mean by "strange"? Simply this—anything enough out of the ordinary to excite you. I have often matched stories (some of them true) with my friends about the unlikely places we've made love. And, believe me, some of them are weird. My little circle of friends has balled girls in the trunk of a 1960 Thunderbird; in the control cabin of a crane; in a helicopter; under the Eiffel Tower; on a tour cruiser down the Seine; on a snowmobile; in the water at St. Tropez (with an audience); on top of a haystack; in the hills above Hollywood with the lights of the city twinkling below; in the bedding section of a department store; on the seventh hole at Indian Wells Golf Course at dusk; on the big rock in front of El Presidente Hotel at night in Acapulco; at the Barbizon Hotel for Women (that was a tough one); on numerous movie sets depicting all periods of time (those are really great because the scene immediately creates a mood and you can let your imagination run wild); in the jungle at Disneyland; in the men's fitting room of Harrod's Department Store in London; on a cable car in the Alps; on the front and back lawns of our homes; and, of course, in numerous swimming pools.

While women may be initially shy about making love in unusual ways and places, once you take the lead and show them how much excitement you can have together, they'll usually be glad to join in the fun and games. The bed is still great, of course, but learn to swing from the chandelier too!

Here are a few adventures you might try:

1. Seek out an isolated spot along a country road some lovely summer evening. Pull up to a grove of trees, park, come around to her side of the car and lift her in your arms (if possible) and carry her into the "forest" (a couple of sheltering trees will do—use your imagination, for Pete's sake). Check the terrain to make sure you're not in someone's back yard, on an army artillery range, or in a patch of poison ivy. When you have determined that the coast is clear, find a soft grassy spot and place a blanket or your jacket on the ground. Remove everything but her skirt (it's more fun that way) and make love to her under the stars. At the moment of climax you will truly be "at one with nature"—just you, she, and the mosquitoes.
2. Another exciting scene—this time in broad daylight—is an almost-isolated beach, prefer-

ably where there are some dunes or tall grass to serve as cover. Remove her bikini, kiss her and caress her passionately, and then go down on her. Imagine the scene: the hot sun, the hot sand, the surf pounding against the shore, and, eventually, you pounding against her. She will get the message. You are telling her that you want her and you don't care if God and the whole *world* are watching—not even the NBC traffic helicopter!

3. Improvise on this experience of mine. I went to play golf late one afternoon and, as it was a slow day at the club, I teamed up with a charming and beautiful lady. Just the two of us in a golf cart with the course almost empty. Naturally, she needed instruction. After I'd put my arms around her three or four times to show her how to make a shot (and inadvertently brushing against her breasts), the juices began to flow. After the fifth hole we ducked into the trees near the green, and she gave me a blow job that left a hitch in my backswing for three months. I reciprocated on the sixth green as dusk was closing in on us; made a "hole-in-one" on the seventh; lost my score card on the eighth; and we've been *great* friends ever since.
4. Even your own home is loaded with erotic potential. The bathtub in particular is one of the most imaginative and yet convenient love

sites you can find. Somehow the privacy we ascribe to our bathrooms becomes charmingly wicked when invaded by two lusty lovers. The beautiful symmetry of a woman's body has always been, to me, the most exciting vision God ever created. With her hair tucked up in a turbanlike towel and her body wet and shining with bubbles and water, she assumes the look of a nymph whose only purpose in life is to please you (if she's in shape, anyway).

In these days of too-small bathtubs, porcelain sex isn't always comfortable, but if you're lucky enough to have a large tub, enjoy it thusly: Use a bubble bath not so intensely aromatic as to overwhelm, and fill the tub three-quarters full of warm water. Settle yourself into the tub first—all the way back—and prop up your rubber ducky on the soap dish. She should now enter the bath, sitting between your legs and leaning back against your chest. With a heavily soaped glove sponge or washcloth, wash and rinse her back, her neck, her breasts, and her pussy with a soft brushing motion, kissing her shoulders and blowing her hair. It's a wonderful time for compliments and playful teasing.

When you are ready (and it won't take you long to be *plenty* ready), she can turn around, facing you, and return the lathering—paying

> careful attention, of course, to your penis, which is drifting dreamily in the suds. Now let the water drain down to about three or four inches. Cushion her head on a small terry-cloth pillow (made for the bath) and then screw her in the bathtub with the rubber ducky looking on. The wet, soapy warmth of her body and the wet, soapy heat inside her cunt will drive you wild. It may also break your back, but it's worth it. I try to do this at least once with every girl I'm dating—and encores are usually the order of the day.

The possibilities for adventurous sex are limitless. Married couples sometimes want to liven up their otherwise routine sex lives by reliving their premarital affairs. They want to taste again those heartstopping moments of stealth when a hotel or motel meant an exciting tryst. Part of the fun is in leaving the wedding rings at home, checking in without luggage, and signing the register "Mr. and Mrs. Smythe." Shacking up in another city is also exciting and can easily be managed on short business trips.

Or you can *fly* together. Night flights have a definite advantage because the lights are out and blankets are available. And experiencing an orgasm while looking *down* on fleecy, moonlit clouds can be a memorable experience. If some of the airlines would promote love-making in first-class seats instead of the trivial gobbledegook they sell now, their flights would be sold out completely. Friendly skies, indeed!

If you're a bit of a voyeur, don't overlook the sensual possibilities of mirrors. By placing mirrors at strategic angles, you can turn your bedroom into a full-color, multi-image erotic environment. Being able to *watch* a beautiful woman bouncing up and down on your erect penis can combine the best features of participation and visual spectacle. Mirrors are *very* erotic and easy to install. The one drawback is that the atmosphere, when the lights are not low, is somewhat akin to that of a barber shop or a men's clothing store. And, if you can't stomach the way you look when you get up in the morning, just buy a hand mirror and fake it.

It is not necessary, remember, to forsake tradition in your quest of adventure and romance. Candlelight and music are still an integral part of the language of love. Whenever possible, provide both. Women love candles. Candlelight enhances their skin tones, heightens their cheekbones, and adds mystery to their eyes. They look their best in candlelight, and they know it (you'll look better yourself). Add the soft music, and you will have conjured up a romantic atmosphere that she will find irresistible. After cocktails, quiet conversation, and preliminary love play, the two of you can fuse together in an atmosphere of soft sensuality.

A bachelor I know in New York has a beautiful duplex apartment overlooking Central Park. I have *never* seen a light on at his place; only the dancing flickers of over one hundred candles. And he is one of the most sought-after guys around (as well as one of the poorest insurance risks).

The candle is the light of love.

17.

Party Sex

Years ago, some ingenious Italian caterer made a brilliant observation at an ancient Roman dinner party. He noticed that, in between grapes, every man was trying to get a peek up the toga of another Roman's wife. And, in between pomegranates, each wife was winking lasciviously to the patrician across the room. Even the slaves, he realized, were horny.

In a burst of inspiration, he hit upon a way

to exploit this delightful situation—and two weeks later he threw, and catered, the first hundred-gold-pieces-a-plate orgy.

The success of the first orgy was spectacular. A wave of wantonness washed across the peninsula. And seven months later, of course, Rome fell.

But nobody cared.

Orgies are still with us today, subsidized and indulged in by the sexually jaded. But I suspect that they are a mere shadow of the original, spectacular Roman variety. How can you compare a garage apartment just off El Camino Real with a Roman temple? How can you compare a seven-buck pair of Levis with a slinky, seductive toga? And how can you expect to top the scandalous carryings-on and unprecedented moral turpitude of those oversexed grape eaters?

You can't. But you can try.

"Orgy" may be too high-class a word to describe typical American party sex, and I hesitate to dignify the average suburban wife-swapper by calling him an "orgiast." (In my opinion, a title like orgiast should only be rewarded after a ten-year apprenticeship, the granting of a high degree, or an appearance on stage at Carnegie Hall.) To the purist, dropping in on the party down the street and just *screwing* everybody isn't enough.

What's that? It *is* enough? Well, maybe you're the sort of guy who would really enjoy party sex. It's mostly a matter of temperament, I guess. I can't keep a straight face at an orgy—a roomful of naked people furiously humping, oblivious to each other's presence, looks a little like the monkey island at the zoo. But, like I said, individual tastes vary.

Naturally, I have drawn up a list of good points and bad points about orgies (I have time to compile these lists because I don't go to many orgies).

Good Points about Orgies

1. Bored married couples can recharge their sexual batteries without resorting to secret, squalid affairs. They can keep an eye on each other at secret, squalid orgies.
2. It can be exciting for the man whose sex life has lacked variety. At an orgy he can do *anything* with *anybody*.
3. The orgy environment can be terrifically stimulating. The sight (and *sound*) of sixteen people fucking can tingle the voyeur in each of us and make our sex that much better.

4. It is honest and uninvolved. Everybody is there for sex, and only sex. You don't have to worry about complicated romantic entanglements. You don't have to make false promises. You don't have to go to the concert with a woman when you hate classical music. All you have to do is pick out what you like—and put your penis in it.
5. You may *learn* something. These people have probably been around. They may show you a new sexual wrinkle or two.
6. You can have all you want—or, at least, all you can stand. Actually, women are better suited for orgies, since they can go on and on and on. But, in any event, it isn't likely you'll go home unsatisfied.
7. It is wonderfully irresponsible. At an orgy, women are usually expected to protect *themselves* when it comes to birth control. Leave your condoms at home unless the invitation specifies "bring your own." Anyway, don't worry about pregnancy. If an orgyette does get knocked up, she'll have a hard time proving which one of nine guys did it to her.
8. It is relatively safe. Since most orgies are held in private homes or apartments, the chances of the police breaking the door down are remote. Of equal concern is the fact that there is little chance of robbery or

mugging, which is always a factor with prostitutes.

9. It can rid you, when you get used to it, of feelings of embarrassment when you are seen naked. Everybody *else* looks so silly that you realize nobody can feel superior to you.
10. The excitement of the orgy can carry over into your regular sex life. A little orgy goes a long way.

Bad Points about Orgies

1. Orgies can take the romance out of sex. There isn't much room for sentiment and involvement at an orgy, and you may find that a steady diet of party sex has robbed you of some of the mystery and suspense that accompany seduction.
2. Not all the women at an orgy are particularly attractive. As at most parties, you'll find all sorts—and you may not want to have sex with *all* sorts. It is wise to go to the orgy with a woman you know you want to fuck—she'll be available if all the other women turn out to be unpalatable.
3. Intimate sexual contact with a dozen or so relative strangers increases the possibility of contracting a venereal disease.

4. You are opening yourself up to blackmail, endangering your professional reputation. And, since many orgiasts are camera enthusiasts, you must always be prepared for that envelope—full of crude black and white prints of you—to show up in your mailbox. (A more startling revelation is when you are watching a stag film at the Elks Lodge and find out that you're *in* it!)
5. You may find that you have been added to some bizarre mailing lists; or you may be subjected to telephone harassment by strange people (stranger, even, than you).
6. You may find yourself part of a sadomasochistic scene that is not really to your taste.
7. Most importantly, you will be contributing to our country's moral decay—and, if America falls, *you* will be held directly responsible.

If you decide that the orgy is for you, be prepared for a long, exhausting evening. Don't go just to *watch*—that's very rude at an orgy. Spread yourself around as far as you will go. That way, nobody will be offended. Don't expect privacy. And don't count on pairing off, because orgiasts love sweaty, heaving, ejaculating heaps of naked bodies (five or six at a time, even!). Wear casual clothes, the kind you can pull off and toss into a corner. And remember, at all times, that you are perpetuating a hallowed tradition in Western civilization.

But, if you get into trouble, don't call on *me* for help. I'll be at home—with one (count her, *one*) woman.

18.

Orgasm—Yours

Most men don't think too much about how they come or why they come. In this chapter I will try to give you a few facts about ejaculation and its relationship to your body and your love-making.

While the woman's orgasmic pleasure during a session of love-making heightens in intensity with each successive orgasm, the man's first orgasm is his most intense and most exciting.

Coming is the height of and the total expression of release on the part of the male, and the initial ejaculation contains the greatest amount of seminal fluid. The woman can feel you come as the fluid is ejected under pressure great enough to shoot one to two feet—if it were not contained within the vagina.

A small sphincter muscle automatically closes off the bladder so there is no intermingling of urine and seminal fluid.

Most men below the age of thirty-three have the ability to ejaculate frequently, so long as they do not adopt the attitude: "I know I can't come again." Given adequate mental and physical stimulation, the male animal can usually come again after a short rest of ten to thirty minutes.

When you have an erection and a small amount of sticky fluid shows at the head of the penis, this is merely the lubricant for the semen which will eventually follow. (However, be careful regarding pregnancy, as even this small amount of fluid is known to carry enough semen for conception.)

One of the greatest fallacies as to what constitutes satisfactory sexual intercourse is the belief that it is important for the male and female to have simultaneous orgasms. Since the lady is multiorgasmic, with each orgasm giving her more pleasure than the previous one, it stands to reason that you should manipulate her to orgasm two, three, five, or ten times before you finally let go. Her added gratification will be the hot feeling of you coming inside her.

Some few men cannot come inside a woman. For psychological reasons, they are unable to ejaculate directly into the vagina, even though they can maintain an erection for an almost unlimited period of time (more than one hour). Psychological help is definitely indicated, as the joy of intercourse will wane as the loving female partner becomes concerned about the problem.

In simple everyday language, what I am saying is the following with respect to normal love-making conditions:

1. The first time you come during a session of love-making is the best, as the amount of fluid you ejaculate is greater than during succeeding orgasms.
2. Since women are multiorgasmic and can come anywhere from ten to fifty times, you can control your ejaculation until you feel you are ready to complete the initial coitus.
3. With proper stimulation, you can come "one more time than you think."
4. Intercourse does not physically weaken a

man. Too many men won't make love to their girl friends or wives the night before a big golf or tennis match. Football players are kept out of the sack by coaches. But if you are in decent physical condition—and you should be for your own sake, there is no proven evidence that intercourse will sap your strength. I play tennis every Sunday morning with one of those guys who won't go near a gal two days before a match. I usually come to the courts right from my girl's bedroom—and I beat him almost every time.

19.

Orgasm—Hers

It pains me to have to say it, but women are the superior sex sexually. They are infinitely more capable of experiencing prolonged pleasure than we are and even have more physical stamina! It may not be too long before women (who are slowly realizing their sexual potential) start treating *us* as sex objects, demanding instant attention and erections and tossing us out if we lose our appeal or don't measure up performancewise.

As discussed in the previous chapter, most males reach orgasm once—maybe twice—in the average evening's love-making. The female, however, can have as many orgasms as she wants—five, ten, fifty, even a hundred—in a single love-making session. All she needs is your cooperation and skilled hands, mouth, and cock. Her orgasms will usually increase in intensity as they progress—the third, for example, being more pleasurable than the first. Women are also capable of multiorgasmic experiences (moving immediately on to a second orgasm while still feeling the effects of the first). And, as if women weren't holding all the trump cards already, recent scientific research has indicated that the female orgasm usually lasts longer than the male.

Now, if all this hasn't left your male ego completely shattered, let me pass on another deflating tidbit: Sex researchers say that the female's most powerful orgasms are achieved through masturbation!

So why do women go to bed with us at all when they can do everything for themselves?

Because for the female, personal involvement is everything. While you, you horny bastard, are capable of jumping into the feathers with practically anything that walks, she wants to know, respect, and feel strong physical attraction toward a man before she heads for the bedroom. A feeling of closeness, tenderness, sensitivity, and love is much more essential to a woman than those strings of orgasms she's so capable of unleashing. (Not that she'll happily settle for closeness and *no* orgasms. The modern female, quite reasonably, expects both.)

It is also quite interesting that most women will receive more pleasure from a medium- or even small-intensity orgasm achieved during love-making than a real blockbuster brought about by masturbation. The lower-caliber orgasm created by you reaffirms her feelings of being an erotic and cherished woman and, of course, that is a *shared* experience.

In the last few years, women have become as hung up on their sexual performance level as men. Men worry about premature ejaculation or not being able to get it up and keep it up, women are panicky if they don't quickly become aroused and if they don't achieve orgasm. It is not at all unusual for the female to need five to ten or even fifteen minutes of stimulation to achieve her first climax. But don't equate a slow starter with unresponsiveness.

Once her body's warmed up, she can continue to attain peaks of excitement indefinitely, remember. And she'll be doing some pretty lively things to you to keep your interest in her pleasure alive.

So even though we're the inferior sex sexually, we're not about to be put out of business. The more sensuous the woman, the more she wants you and will do anything to keep you as a lover. That's not such a bad deal if you think about it.

Maybe one day, if we all become great lovers, *we'll* get the alimony.

20.

Love as an Aphrodisiac

How do I love thee? Let me count the ways.
I love thee to the depth and breadth and height
My soul can reach, when feeling out of sight
For the ends of Being and ideal Grace.
I love thee to the level of every day's
Most quiet need, by sun and candle-light.
I love thee freely, as men strive for Right;
I love thee purely, as they turn from Praise.
I love thee with the passion put to use
In my old griefs, and with my childhood's faith.

I love thee with a love I seemed to lose
With my lost saints,—I love thee with the
breath, Smiles, tears, of all my life!—and,
if God choose, I shall but love thee better after
death.
—Elizabeth Barrett Browning (1850)

I've never read anything anywhere that says "I love you" better than that. Love transcends all of our catting around and creates a feeling so fantastic as to make us think of past sexual forays as mild encounters. Love makes us float instead of walk. We laugh on trains and in busses, and everyone smiles with us. We want to open our arms and our hearts to the whole world to show the wonderful feeling bursting inside us, and we wrap every waking moment into a daydream of the way she looks and feels and smells and sounds, until she is once again in our arms—and the dream is reality.

Love also makes the blood pound faster and faster. You can't keep your hands off her. You want to kiss every inch of her, from top to bottom and all around. You want to fuck her for hours and days and weeks unending until you die in each other's arms. And you want to do it again and again and again.

Jim Moran said in his book, *Why Men Shouldn't Marry,* that "Love is a form of temporary insanity," and so it is. Men have committed suicide, robbed, murdered, jumped off bridges, and fought for love.

If we're capable of doing all that, imagine how tremendous is our drive to satisfy the woman who is the object of that desire!

I want you, I want you, I want you is the battle cry. And I will do anything to make you happy. It's glorious. Don't be a fool. Take advantage of it in every way, shape, and form. It doesn't come that often. Perhaps just once in a lifetime. You can love many times, but rarely are you "in love."

It is a time of erotic feeling beyond the limits of imagination. Her eyes are stars, her lips are petals. Her neck is swanlike, her breasts are mounds of pure alabaster pliant to your touch, her waist is a wisp of flesh warm and smooth, her buttocks are solid to the pressure of your hands, and her cunt is the altar at which you pray. It is the ultimate area of her totality as a woman to which you are inescapably drawn and, as your tongue and your lips bring forth from it a hot torrent of love juices, the tears of joy to tell you she loves you, you join her, thrusting deeply into the fountain, twisting, pushing, holding, kissing, until the world moves far away and only two spent, happily ecstatic lovers are left alone floating somewhere on a cloud.

I love all women, but there is only one love.

Conclusion

Every book should have an orgasm. That last chapter was mine—a literary ejaculation that conveys, to the best of my ability, the way I feel about love and sex. As Elizabeth Browning says, they are "out of sight."

Now, basking in the afterglow of writing a book, I find that I've had a better time writing it than I ever expected. It was far from drudgery, and I hope my enthusiasm was contagious.

My moods are mercurial, I know. I mock one moment, preach another, and rhapsodize the next. But I don't apologize for it. That's what sex is like—warm, ecstatic, ludicrous, unfathomable, and exciting. Sex is the original paradox, utterly trivial or the only thing in life that matters, depending on the time and place.

My last words on the subject, then, are these: Sex is love and sex is life. If my writing has contributed to your appreciation of that fact, then my effort has been well worth while.

Good luck to you. I've written enough, and it's time you were off somewhere *doing* the things I've described in *The Sensuous Man.*

And I think it's time I did the same. May your every orgasm surpass the last!